THE UNOFFICIAL GAY MANUAL

KEVIN DILALLO
AND JACK KRUMHOLTZ

with contributions and illustrations by
Robert Hickey

and contributions and photographs by
David MacKay

A MAIN STREET BOOK

NEW YORK   LONDON   TORONTO   SYDNEY   AUCKLAND

THE UNOFFICIAL GAY MANUAL

Living the Lifestyle

Or at Least Appearing To

A MAIN STREET BOOK
PUBLISHED BY DOUBLEDAY
a division of
Bantam Doubleday Dell Publishing Group, Inc.
1540 Broadway, New York, New York 10036

MAIN STREET BOOKS, DOUBLEDAY, and the portrayal of a building
with a tree are trademarks of Doubleday, a division of
Bantam Doubleday Dell Publishing Group, Inc.

STOCK PORTRAIT CREDITS

Portraits of James Baldwin, Gaius Julius Caesar, Voltaire,
Sigmund Freud, reprinted with permission of Archive Photos.

Portraits of James Buchanan (engraving by John C. Buttre) and Walt Whitman
are reproduced from *Dictionary of American Portraits,* Dover Publications, Inc.
(New York, 1967).

Portrait of Edward II reprinted with permission of Everett/CSU Archives.

Portrait of Rudolph Valentino reprinted with permission of
Archive Photos/American Stock Photo.

Certain quotations reprinted with permission from Companion Publications,
P.O. Box 2575, Laguna Hills, California 92654. Copyright © 1994 Steve Stewart.
All rights reserved.

Certain quotations reprinted with permission from Alyson Publications, Inc.,
40 Plympton St., Boston, Massachusetts 02118. Copyright © 1988 Leigh Rutledge.
All rights reserved.

Library of Congress Cataloging-in-Publication Data
DiLallo, Kevin.
    The unofficial gay manual: living the lifestyle or at least appearing to / Kevin
DiLallo and Jack Krumholtz; with contributions and illustrations by Robert Hickey
and contributions and photographs by David MacKay. — 1st ed.
        p.   cm.
    "A Main Street book."
    1. Gay men—United States.   2. Gay men—United States—Humor.
I. Krumholtz, Jack.   II. Title.
HQ76.3.U5D55   1994
305.38'9664'0973—dc20   94-10769
                                                                    CIP

ISBN 0-385-47445-8

10   9   8   7   6

ACKNOWLEDGMENTS

We owe a great deal of gratitude to the many people who helped to make *The Unofficial Gay Manual* possible. First and foremost, we would like to thank Robert Hickey, our illustrator, and David MacKay, our photographer, for their untiring dedication to this project, their creative insights into gay culture, and most of all their patience with our compulsive approach to deadlines. Much appreciation also goes to our agent Sloan Harris and editor Bruce Tracy—Sloan for seeing the art of the possible and Bruce for helping us choose the right colors, strokes, and subjects for our portrait of gay life.

A picture truly is worth a thousand words, and this effort would have far less personal appeal without the help of so many friends, gay or merely just enlightened, willing to throw caution to the wind and appear in the *Manual*. Their continued good humor and patience through constant costume changes and reshoots are the stuff of which years of fond memories are made. Specifically, heartfelt thanks go to Paul B., Marie Berliner, Bert the Dog, Bruce G. Bonn, M.D., Claude P. Boudrias, Scott Brinitzer, Stephen Brown, Sean Bugg, Keith Cohn, David M. Cox, Bernie Cummings, Destiny, Jeffrey DiLallo, Barry Dixon, Ms. Domurot, Eddie the Pup, Erwin (who not only went in front of the camera but made the rest of us look our best before we did), Joyce Felton, Chotima Harris, Heinie, Brian Hujdich, Ernie Johnston, Susan H. R. Jones, Erica Kane (Miss Gay D.C.), Carroll LeTellier, Jr., Sally Lund, Sam Marsh, Meg, Tim Miller, Christopher Murphy (clothes by Christopher Murphy for Christopher Black), Fred W. Pagan, Dave Parham, David Park, Michael Richard, Warren Rickart, Chris Riss, Steve Russell, Michael Schmidt, Greg Stitz, Rich Sullivan, Courtney Taylor, and Eddie H. Whitehurst.

All the books we read and all the research we did couldn't match the information, ideas, and anecdotes offered by the many friends, new and old, who served as our correspondents on gay life all over the country, or who just offered useful general advice and ideas. In particular, we owe a profound debt to Robert Alexander, Stephen Brown, Bernie Cummings, Mark H. Cunningham, C³—Cutest Closet Case, Cutest Gay Baby, Beverly DiLallo, Jeffrey DiLallo, John Emanuelson, Freeman

Fisher, Friends of the Pig, Heinie, Maria Herrmann, Bruce Hodges, Andrew Isen, Ernie Johnston, George Knod, Rob Lopardo, MVL, Sam Marsh, Jim McDonough, Charlie McKnight, John Nolan, Connie O'Shaughnessy, JMR, RFDQ, Chris Riss, Kelly S., Sean Sheer, Randy Shorr, Sly, Gene C. Sulzberger, RHS, Steve Russell, DFT, David Taylor, David White, Pat Whittle, and Richard Wortman. We also would like to thank the dozens of hotline operators who answered our calls and our questions with humor and good sense.

We are grateful to Leigh Rutledge and Alyson Publications, Inc., author and publisher of *Unnatural Quotations*, and Steve Stewart and Companion Publications, author and publisher of *Gay Hollywood Film & Video Guide*, which pointed us to many of the noteworthy quotations used in the book.

Finally, we would like to thank the friends and family members who offered words of encouragement as we wrote the *Manual,* and our employers, for having a sense of humor. Their enthusiasm and support for this project helped us make it through the many times when we wondered what in the hell we had gotten ourselves into.

CONTENTS

To our families

THE UNOFFICIAL GAY MANUAL

FOREWORD

"... [I]f you removed all of the homosexuals and homosexual influence from what is generally regarded as American culture, you would pretty much be left with *Let's Make a Deal*."

—FRAN LEBOWITZ

After centuries of persecution and life in the closet, it's finally, on the eve of the Millennium, okay—even cool—to be gay. It's about *time.*

But what does "gay" mean? A lot more than just hopping in the sack with someone of the same sex, to be gay is to live in two worlds at the same time: the ordinary world that most people know, and the gay world, an extraordinary place populated with talented, interesting, and often outrageous characters with an uncanny knack for thoughtful accessorizing.

Above all, "gay" is a way of life; the gay world has its own vocabulary, customs, and rules for living. Gays are the high priests of trends, taste, and tans. Name a trend, and chances are that gays played a big role in launching it. A world without gays would be a world without braided belts or body building; Swatches or slipper chairs; torn jeans or track lighting. And, if it weren't for the support of their gay fans, Madonna, Midler, and Minnelli would be singing "Feelings" in some Marriott cocktail lounge. Gays have contributed more to society than most people realize: Imagine a world without the Sistine Chapel, *Anything Goes,* or *Moby-Dick*—all creations of gay men. Yet, for all their contributions and influence, gays have been underappreciated since the fall of the Roman Empire.

What makes gays so special? It could be the freedom that comes when you accept the fact that you're a member of the last minority group it's still acceptable to hate, at least in some quarters. If you can deal with that, you can deal with anything—except perhaps bad taste. Gays are willing to try anything, and their sense of adventure is heightened by an insatiable appetite for new things, new experiences, and new friends and lovers. But behind all that's new are many constants—indeed, standards—in the gay world.

Go into any gay man's home and chances are he'll have many of the same albums, books, and magazines as his counterparts elsewhere in the country. Most likely the home will be discerningly decorated and stylish clothes will be hanging in the closet. The man's dating habits, from cruising and meeting men to the mating ritual and nesting, will parallel those of his brothers living from coast to coast. And when he speaks of Judy, his friends will all know he means Garland.

This is not to say that gay culture is homogeneous—far from it. Although they're both denizens of the gay world, Poodles and Gym Dandies have about as much in common (at least on the surface) as Baptists and Buddhists. And the gay world would be a pretty boring place if there weren't scantily clad, hedonistic Club Kids to shock and tantalize staid, buttoned-down A-Listers. Yet, beneath their superficial differences, all gay men share common experiences, from the evolution of self-realization to coming out and living in two worlds that don't intersect as often as they should.

The Unofficial Gay Manual is a humorous lifestyle guide to the gay world, for men who are, men who could, and men who should be gay. The *Manual* spans the gay experience: from the roots and causes of being gay to the gay equivalent of big game hunting—looking for a lover; from coming out to the dangers of overexposure; and from perfecting your own individual image to living the lifestyle to the fullest.

A few words about the scope of the *Manual:* First, we don't pretend to know much about our stouthearted sisters with the good throwing arms; thus, we've stayed within the limits of our own experience. Second, the *Manual* says little about AIDS. This is because the *Manual* is a humor book, and there's nothing funny about AIDS.

The reader may ask how the authors researched this book.

Primarily, we lived it. Indeed, we live it (and love it) every day. And we hope that everyone—whether a gay man or not—will gain a greater appreciation of our culture from reading *The Unofficial Gay Manual.*

Kevin DiLallo
Jack Krumholtz

CHAPTER I
BECOMING GAY
Environment, Heredity, or Just Plain Luck?

Gay (gā) *adj.* **A. 1.** Of persons, their attributes and actions: Full of or disposed to joy and mirth; light-hearted, exuberantly cheerful, sportive, merry. **1843** LYTTON, *Last Bar.* 1. i. Edward was the handsomest, the gayest, and the bravest prince in Christendom. **1789**, W. BUCHAN, *Dom. Med.* (1790) 89 That greatest of human blessings [sleep] . . . visits the happy, the cheerful, and the gay.

2. Addicted to social pleasures and dissipations. Often *euphemistically:* Of loose or immoral life. **1851** MAYHEW, *Lond. Labour* I. 382 The principal of the firm was what is termed "gay." He was particularly fond of attending public entertainments. **1891** E. PEACOCK, *N. Brendon* I. 302 This elder Narcissa had led a gay and wild life while beauty lasted.

3. Bright or lively-looking, esp. in colour; brilliant, showy.

4. Finely or showily dressed.

5. In immaterial sense: Brilliant, attractive, charming.

6. Brilliantly good; excellent, fine.*

*Excerpted from *The Oxford English Dictionary* (Oxford University Press, 1971).

4

WHY SOME MEN CAN ARRANGE FLOWERS AND OTHERS CAN'T

"I ascertain that I'm homosexual. OK. That's no cause for alarm. How and why are idle questions. A little like my wanting to know why my eyes are green."

—JEAN GENET

Since the dawn of time, Man has wondered where he came from. In that respect, gay men are no different than anyone else. So why do some boys turn out straight and others grow up with an innate ability to throw dinner parties? Is it heredity or caused by some tiny gland behind the left ear? Religious fundamentalists may preach that it's a choice, or the result of masturbation; but if that were the case, everyone would be gay. Those who thrive on guilt—you know who you are—often blame the parents (either the domineering mother or the distant father). And alarmists may point to the friendly pastor, scoutmaster, or other male authority figure who took a particular interest in a young man's life. Although these theories still enjoy shockingly broad currency, they have about as much substance as a G-string from International Male. Yet, in the pursuit of knowledge, the leading theories are reviewed below:

Myth #1: The Domineering Mother

"I have been perfectly happy the way I am. If my mother was responsible for it, I am grateful."
—CHRISTOPHER ISHERWOOD

Take one part Joan Crawford, one part Donna Reed, and one part Mussolini, blanch, strain, and you've got the Domineering Mother.

A domineering mother knows what's best for her pride and joy and what's not. In fact, the domineering mother often knows what's best for everyone. She's the first mom to volunteer to be the cookie-baking room mother—what better way to keep an eye on little Bruce and score brownie points for him with the teacher. She spends more time behind the wheel than a Teamster, what with Boy Scouts, little league practice, school plays, and Sunday school. Later in life, she makes her son her sole confidant and expects to be his. And the whole time, she reminds him of the sacrifices she's made—not for her benefit, of course, but to guarantee *his* success.

Proponents of this theory contend that the domineering mother tries to shape her son in her own image, at least as she would have wanted to be if she were a boy. If she pushes too hard, so the theory goes, instead of *marrying* a girl like dear old mom, he'll *become* a "girl" just like her. Rather than collecting baseball cards and watching sports, he'll collect chinoiserie and watch Bette Davis movies.

Experience teaches that the correlation between the domineering mother and gay life is purely coincidental. Plenty of men grow up with domineering mothers and turn out completely straight. Homicidal maniacs, but straight. And many a gay man grows up with quiet, homespun moms and winds up sporting Ethel Merman drag and belting out "There's No Business Like Show Business" in some piano bar. So, on to the next theory.

Myth #2: The Distant Father

"I can be butch when I have to—I get it from my mother."

—PETER FRIEDMAN, IN *SINGLE WHITE FEMALE*

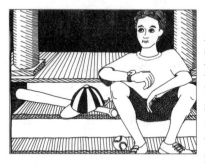

While the departure of the American family from the Ozzie and Harriet model has had some positive results (e.g., the increasing acceptance of nontraditional families), it's also had its drawbacks. Among these is the growing absence of fathers from the family circle. Armchair psychologists have hypothesized that distant dads leave their sons without positive male role models, resulting in guys who don't know how to "be a man."

One basic flaw with this theory is that gays recognize at an early age that a gay man who doesn't know how to "be a man" is like a fish that can't swim. Almost anybody can butch it up if necessary, but gay men realize that, to be a *real* man takes courage, integrity, and self-respect. If these traits aren't instilled at home, gay men learn them soon enough in the classroom of life.

Another flaw in the absent father theory is that, unfortunately, a substantial number of households are fatherless. Odds are, all the kids from these homes won't turn out gay, though that remains to be seen. This may still be a straight male-dominated society, but the sins of our fathers and their influence on us have been greatly overestimated. If not, we'd all be wearing Old Spice. Absent dads shouldn't blame themselves for their sons' turning out gay. Their sons have it all: They're as much a man as anyone else, and more woman than dear old dad could ever handle. So much for armchair psychology.

Myth #3: The Friendly Pastor and Other Authority Figures

> "There is no need for parents to fear homosexual teachers. Ninety-seven percent of child seduction is heterosexual."
>
> **—DR. BENJAMIN SPOCK**

Despite recurring revelations about priestly indiscretions, it's not fair to lay blame for Jonathan's proclivities at the feet of Father Matthew or some other male role model in Jonathan's life. But parents of gay men, finding a worn copy of *The Front Runner* under their sons' mattresses, often curse themselves for encouraging their sons to be altar boys or pushing them to get involved in after-school activities—the Boy Scouts, the football team, band, and especially drama. How could they have been so naive? they ask themselves. Naive, indeed.

What these parents fail to grasp is that Jonathan's interest in extracurricular activities stems less from his admiration for the male sponsors than from his affinity for the fabulous accoutrements involved. A few cases in point: the altar boy—sanctioned, prepubescent drag; the Boy Scouts—early indication of a uniform fetish; the football team—a yearning for broad shoulders; and drama—all that makeup . . . Enough said.

But what if the priest, scoutmaster, or coach makes an untoward advance? Traumatic and potentially damaging, such an overture would be enough to drive even the most curious youngster hopelessly into the closet, *not* inspire him to "sing in the choir." And in any event it's more likely that the drama teacher spent all that extra time helping Jonathan learn his lines because his Gaydar told him that Jonathan could use a positive gay role model, not because of improper motives.

There *are* plenty of straight band teachers, scoutmasters, and priests, or so it's said. And those that aren't would rather spend their free time with real men, not boys. So it's probably a stretch to say that Coach Johnson's tender loving care massaging the cramp in nubile Jon's leg had anything to do with the fact that Jonathan is now working the Hermès counter at Saks. Even if Coach Johnson *is* his best customer.

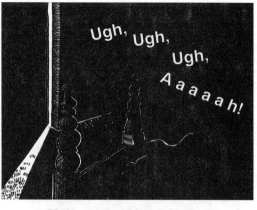

Myth #4: Masturbation

Oh, puh-leeeeeze. Not *everybody's* gay, are they?

"It's just a phase you're going through. Last year it was miniature golf."

—KAYE BALLARD, IN *THE RITZ*

The Truth: Just Plain Luck

For gay men, it's not only what's in the *jeans* that matters (and it *does* matter), it's also what's in the *genes*. Research indicates that, as with eye and hair color, there may be a genetic basis for that certain impulse which, if acted on, makes gays outlaws in many states and disqualifies them from military service. (Hardly sounds fair, does it?) But why do some baby boys get the gene and others don't? Someone has to perpetuate the race.

Whether you respond when you get that fateful wake-up call from Mother Nature (probably a lesbian) is another matter. The real question is not what makes you gay, but what gives you the courage to act on it. This is where environment comes in. The truth is: It's tough being gay, at least at first. Who wants to be called a "faggot" by his schoolmates? But as your self-confidence develops, the fear of rejection gives way to the desire to be true to yourself. This is undoubtedly why so many gay men are over-achievers. "If I'm better than anyone else at something—or everything—the fact that I'm gay won't matter."

For those who can't seem to nudge that closet door open and see the light of day, take heart: Times and attitudes are changing. Things may still not be ideal, but they're better now than they were twenty years ago, and a hell of a lot better than they were before that. The trick is to make the best of it, and showing you how is one of the purposes of this book.

IS YOUR YOUNGER BROTHER (OR NEPHEW) GAY?

How can you tell if your younger brother or nephew is going to turn out gay? Why should you care? Experience tells us that there's no single path that all young boys take toward becoming gay, no conclusive telltale sign or particular trait. A preference for musical theater over touch football (or vice versa) does not necessarily a gay man make. Consider the following boys:

PROFILE ONE: THE SENSITIVE CHILD
1. Picks out own clothes.
2. Has memorized the words from "Oklahoma!"
3. Hates dirty fingernails.
4. Writes letters to grandparents.
5. Many girl *friends*.
6. Knows the moves for the fox-trot.
7. Opts out of gym class.
8. National Merit Scholar.

AFTER COMING OUT:
1. Wears hospital scrubs outside of work.
2. Has library of PBS specials on video.
3. Takes tennis lessons.
4. Subscribes to *National Geographic*.
5. Is in the gay running club.
6. Shops at Barneys for clothes seen in *GQ*.
7. Keeps Randy Shilts on the coffee table.
8. Has a personal trainer at the gym.

PROFILE TWO: THE JOCK
1. Picks clothes out of the hamper.
2. Has memorized National League batting averages.
3. Has dirt behind his ears.
4. Letters in basketball.
5. Many *girlfriends*.
6. Knows the moves for a halfback option.
7. Plays locker room pranks.
8. Eagle Scout.

AFTER COMING OUT:
1. Wears Calvin Klein underwear on the outside.
2. Has complete collection of porn classics.
3. Teaches aerobics.
4. Reads *People* in the checkout line.
5. Frequents the J.O. club.
6. Orders from International Male.
7. Has dog-eared Jackie Collins on the nightstand.
8. Hangs out in the steam room.

TEN REASONS TO FEEL LUCKY TO HAVE A GAY CHILD

Some say there's at least a one-in-ten chance that a boy will grow up gay. For those parents who need a reason to feel lucky to have a gay son, here are ten:

1. Whatever he does, he'll do his best.

2. He'll be a good son, especially in your old age.

3. He'll be an interesting conversationalist, an excellent addition to parties.

4. Either he or his lover will be a fabulous cook and a great host for the holidays.

5. He'll always be available as a fourth for bridge.

6. He'll buy you thoughtful and tasteful gifts. (He knows the difference between Meissen and Mikasa.)

7. He'll clue you in to the latest restaurants, plays, movies, and celebrity gossip.

8. He'll be a handy (and free) consultant for weddings, parties, decorating, and wardrobe.

9. No danger of disagreeable daughters-in-law.

10. When he's older, he'll never be lonely, because for years he'll have cultivated a wide circle of close, caring friends.

If this list makes straight readers wish they had a gay relative, take heart: You probably do.

HIDING YOUR LIGHT UNDER A BUSHEL

In the Sermon on the Mount, Jesus encouraged his follow-ers not to hide their lights under a bushel (Matthew 5: 14–16), and that advice is still good today. Still, it's amazing what some guys will do to avoid confronting their destiny. Some of those who can't (or won't) see the writing on the wall waste their time looking desperately for Ms. Goodbar. Eventually, they may end up married, but only for money, social standing, or fear of the *alternative*. Others throw in the towel and settle into a steady relationship with a little imagination and their right hand. Some of these eventually join the clergy. The real social deviants overcompensate for their self-perceived "short-coming" and become professed homophobes.

Arrested Development: Homophobia and Other Forms of Over-Compensation

History is full of them: Roy Cohn, J. Edgar Hoover, Terry Dolan. Homo homophobes think they have the rest of the world fooled, but they really don't. They talk a big, tough game, but inside they want nothing more than to cuddle up with the boy next door. And that scares the hell out of them. The message to these guys is clear: Get over it.

Of all the paths facing a gay man, homophobia is perhaps the most treacherous. Many of us have witnessed a professed homophobe's forced inappropriate remarks about the anatomy of the opposite sex, or his distasteful jokes at the expense of his true brethren. The sad truth is that the self-loathing the homophobe feels is tenfold the hate he displays toward others. Honey, it just isn't worth it. For those who find themselves in this disagreeable phase, hope that it's just that—a phase. To thine own self be true.

Avoidance 101: Contemplating the Clergy

There seems to be a certain affinity between gays and the clergy. The attraction is anybody's guess: The clothes are unflattering and, if you're Catholic, just think how long you'll have to wait to wear red. Worst of all, sex is often *verboten.* So what's to like? Based on informal observations, it seems that some men who become men of the cloth do so because they are really men of the closet, and want to stay that way. Mother Church (there's that domineering mother again) will keep them in that closet. Won't she?

Of course, there is the pomp and circumstance associated with so many religions, and more than a few gay men harbor the fantasy of walking down the aisle in a fabulous gown (or robe). But without a true calling (and there are many gay religious organizations for those with that calling), all the incense and organ music in the world can't keep that closet door closed. Be it divine intervention or some cosmic prank, gay men must play the hand they're dealt. If a clerical collar is in the cards, then Godspeed. If not, don't cloister your true light in some monastery, but help others by first helping yourself and staying in the game.

Avoidance 102: Get Me to the Church on Time

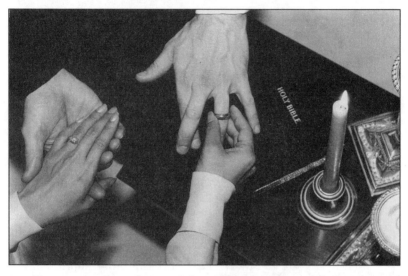

For some gays who can't bear the thought of themselves in black cassocks and chastity belts, the preferred alternative (though far from perfect) is a simple band of gold. Gays who marry often think that their wives can come between them and their true selves. If only it were that simple.

Despite best intentions, gays who cross their fingers and think they can make a heterosexual marriage work are doing no one any good, particularly not the unfortunate women they marry. Sooner or later, their hormones will likely get the best of them. And few women have the patience or lack of self-respect to be ladies in waiting while their confused husbands sort things out. Those that do deserve a Purple Heart or perhaps a good therapist.

So why do some gay men choose a traditional marriage? Maybe because of perceived family, social, or religious pressures. But what could be worse than not living the life you were meant to live? Receiving fifteen place settings of Royal Doulton and only three of Waterford stemware, for starters. That would *never* happen at a gay wedding.

TEN CLUES THAT THE NEW GUY IN THE OFFICE IS GAY

It's a common scenario: A new guy starts at the office, attractive and outgoing. Before they even know his name, some of his female co-workers will want to know "Is he married? Is he seeing someone?" To avoid abject humiliation, women who *have* to know should look for certain clues before pursuing the guy in the office next door:

1. He lives in town.

2. He's perpetually tan.

3. He's over thirty and still single.

4. He has chosen art posters for his office walls.

5. He receives many calls from men, but there are few messages from women.

6. On Monday mornings, he vaguely says that he "went out with friends" over the weekend.

7. He compliments women on their outfits, and always has a perfect dimple in his tie.

8. He doesn't enter the office football pool but always picks the Oscar winners.

9. He knows the waiters at all the "in" restaurants in town.

10. He works harder than most.

Ultimately, no manner of detours or denials will steer gay men from their true course. The lifestyle may be inconvenient and even difficult at times, but it's worth it. The gay world is much more than a loose collection of "lighthearted, exuberantly cheerful, sportive, and merry" chaps who can name every Rodgers & Hammerstein musical; it's a cohesive community with interesting and diverse inhabitants who add distinctive spice to the universal melting pot. This Man*ual* is a guide to that world.

CHAPTER II

JUNE IS BUSTING OUT ALL OVER
Coming Out

"One should never lose hope. Homosexuality can strike any straight man at any age."
—ROGER PEYREFITTE (FRENCH NOVELIST)

Coming out is no debutante ball. There are no corsages or long white gloves, no ceremonies with handsome escorts in tails, no greeting cards with checks from aunts and uncles.

Coming out is a process, an evolution. Years may pass between a guy's first gay encounter and the eventual disclosure to family and friends that his "roommate" Kevin doesn't really sleep on the hide-a-bed in the living room.

Whether you're keenly aware of it, or just have a nagging feeling that something's not quite "right," there are certain unmistakable signs that you're not in Kansas anymore. In the overall cosmic scheme, it may be one small step for mankind, but it's a hell of a leap for you. Being able to recognize the signs could mean the difference between a smooth journey to Oz or being hit in the head by a farmhouse. For those about to be clobbered, a short self-test:

Is the Inevitable About to Happen?

"What happened to you? You used to be normal."
"I grew out of it."
—KENNETH MCMILLAN AND AIDAN QUINN, IN *RECKLESS*

INSTRUCTIONS: *Indicate whether each statement below is True or False. Points are provided, and the answers appear below. If you score 30 points or less, don't try to redecorate your place without first consulting a professional; between 30 and 90 points, you may be surprised at how naturally you can quote Bette Davis at appropriate times; a score of 90 or higher qualifies you as an official F.O.D. ("Friend of Dorothy"). Congratulations!*

1. Mousse is an essential part of your grooming routine. *10 points.*
   T__ F__

2. Joseph Aboud is a Middle Eastern diplomat. *10 points.*
   T__ F__

3. Your girlfriends dance better than you do. *10 points.*
   T__ F__

4. You subscribe to *GQ* or *Men's Fitness. 10 points.*
   T__ F__

5. Madonna is a religious figure. *10 points.*
   T__ F__

6. The primary goal of working out is to build strength *15 points.*
   T__ F__

7. International Male is a travel magazine. *15 points.*
   T__ F__

8. Bronzer is something for shining tarnished metal objects. *15 points.*
   T__ F__

9. Bruce Weber won a gold medal in the Olympics. *15 points.*
   T__ F__

10. When buying greeting cards, you linger over the cards with half-naked men. *15 points.*
    T__ F__

11. You ignore the knowing stares you receive from waiters while you're dining. *20 points.*
    T__ F__

12. Marky Mark is best known for his singing ability. *15 points.*
    T__ F__

13. When having people over for dinner, you serve a dish made with any of the following: (1) Cool Whip; (2) miniature marshmallows; (3) canned cream of mushroom soup; and/or (4) Velveeta. *20 points.*
    T__ F__

14. When watching a football game, you leave the room during the razor blade ads. *20 points.*
    T__ F__

15. Disco is dead. *20 points.*
    T__ F__

ANSWERS:
1. **True.** No grooming routine would be complete without it, unless, of course, you use gel, sculpting lotion, or a similar product (or you're bald).
2. **False.** Where do you buy your clothes?
3. **False.** If so, give Arthur Murray a call. Some people still think you

can tell how good a guy is in the bedroom by the way he moves on the dance floor.

4. **True.** And the clothes and workout tips aren't the only reason you buy them.

5. **False.** No blasphemy intended. If you missed this one, you're not only hopelessly straight, but you've been living under a rock for the past ten years.

6. **False.** Maybe if you're a professional athlete, or work for a moving company. But for most, the primary—okay, only—goal of working out is to look good on the beach. It's a jungle out there.

7. **False.** It's the gay man's equivalent of the Victoria's Secret catalog, but the clothes are more revealing *and* are meant to be worn in public.

8. **False.** Okay, bronzer may be a step or two away from eyeliner, but come January, it's a godsend.

9. **False.** Not unless they've made photographing beefcake an Olympic event.

10. **True.** Add 15 points if you actually had the nerve to buy one; subtract 10 points if it was for your girlfriend.

11. **False.** It may be a little unnerving at first, but take it as a compliment. Who knows? You might even get a cappuccino on the house.

12. **False.** He can sing?

13. **False.** The only person who can get away with eating like this anymore is Bill Clinton.

14. **False.** Are you kidding? The shaving ads show you what every gay man dreams of waking up to in the morning.

15. **False.** If you think disco went out with *Saturday Night Fever,* you've spent too many Saturday nights watching bad sitcoms. It may have evolved into "dance music," but the beat goes on.

"With the right wine and the right music there're damn few that aren't curious."

**—LARRY, FROM *THE BOYS IN THE BAND*,
BY MART CROWLEY**

TEN SIGNALS THAT YOU'RE THE OBJECT OF DESIRE

The first time it happens, you may think you're imagining things. Does that guy following you around the grocery store want something? You bet he does, and if you're not interested, stop turning around to look at him. In time, you'll learn.

1. The same guy is at the gym whenever you are, and seems to follow your routine.

2. You receive more hang-up calls than usual.

3. The male flight attendant offers you free (and strong) drinks, or the florist gives you extra flowers.

4. The guy you pass on the street every morning gives you a strangely knowing look.

5. A new male friend asks if you're dating anyone.

6. Although you've gone to the same clothing store for years, the salesman measures your inseam each time.

7. A male friend suggests that the two of you go on a vacation together—alone.

8. You're invited to a party, and arrive only to find that it's all men.

9. You go to the movies with a guy and he "inadvertently" puts his hand on your knee during the film.

10. You think you're being followed, and you are.

A CARDINAL COMING OUT RULE

Whether you're the game or the game warden, there is one cardinal rule which all novitiates must follow: Don't be stupid. It may work into your plan to *act* as if you're drunk and don't know what you're doing, but don't let alcohol or anything else impair your good judgment. You are blessed with a wonderful gift. Your first time should be the beginning of a lifetime of warmth, wit, and wonder; don't let it be the beginning of the end. *Practice safe sex.* For more information, call your local gay men's health clinic or hotline.

The Morning After: Coming to Grips with It

> "It is better to be hated for what one is than loved for what one is not."
>
> **—ANDRÉ GIDE (FRENCH WRITER)**

Awkward as it may have been—and it's often *so* awkward—gay men will always remember their first time. Whether they've endured years of tortured self-doubt before experiencing their sexual epiphany or had it come upon them suddenly, like a Mack truck without brakes, most gay men will be telling and retelling the story of their first encounter for years after the fact. Over time, reality may give way to embellishment, and the blessed event will soon rival the Big Bang.

Once you've taken the leap, what's next? Cosmetology school? Fortunately, that's not your only option. Being gay doesn't mean you have to conform to anyone's idea of what gay is. For every Paul Lynde and Truman Capote out there, there's a Joseph Steffan and Bob Jackson-Paris. The stereotypical "fairy" is as mythical as the straight guy who can dance. Being gay doesn't prevent you from achieving anything you want, unless *you* let it.

From the very beginning, the most important questions a gay man will face are whether to come out, when, how far, and to whom. The answers aren't always simple.

Option #1: Life Behind the Closet Door

> "How can sleeping with a woman make you proud of yourself if you know you'd rather be with a man?"
> **—HARVEY FIERSTEIN, IN** *TORCH SONG TRILOGY*

The majority of gay men don't go directly from their first time to leading the local Gay Pride parade. For most, it's a long way from the dark, fearful recesses of their own minds to the light of day.

Coming out carries with it so many complications (or so it seems): family expectations, religious taboos, work-related repercussions, and general public disapproval. The decision whether to go public becomes one of balancing your own peace of mind against the risk of negative reactions. In the long run, it's a very personal decision, and one which others should respect. Don't be bullied into coming out until *you're* ready.

Coming out may have its drawbacks, but they pale in comparison to the complications associated with life in the closet. For those weighing the pros and cons of putting their lives in mothballs, consider these:

PROS:
1. You're invited to a lot of straight parties.
2. You meet many nice, single women.
3. You're often asked to play golf.
4. You're invited to a lot of weddings.

5. There's less pressure to stay in shape or keep yourself looking sharp.
6. There's security in not taking risks.

CONS:
1. Straight parties can be boring as hell.
2. You know enough women. You want to meet *men*.
3. You hate golf.
4. Weddings are expensive, and odds are *you'll* never be on the receiving end (at least for gifts).
5. Who wants to look like Rush Limbaugh or Howard Stern?
6. If you don't play the lottery, you'll never win the jackpot.

Option #2: A Brave New World

"If a caterpillar was afraid of wings, it would never become a butterfly, and people would say, 'Hey, look, it's a worm in a tree.'"
—HOLLIS McLAREN, IN *OUTRAGEOUS!*

To those guys courageous enough to throw caution to the winds and fling open that closet door: Welcome to a brave new world. Most people aren't that well acquainted with the mainstream world (what *is* the capital of Madagascar, anyway?), much less the gay world. For the record, some facts and figures:

Ten Percent? (Facts and Figures of Gay America)

No one really knows what percentage of the population is gay and lesbian. Estimates range from 1 to 20 percent, but reliable data are hard to come by. One problem is that sexual orientation is thought not to be a black-or-white, either/or matter, but a continuum. And since those who confine themselves to their closets are unlikely to open the door to their friendly census taker, it's safe to assume that any "official" estimate will be low. It *has* been estimated that there are at least 18 million gay and lesbian Americans; and 10 percent of those responding to a 1985 telephone poll by the *Los Angeles Times* identified themselves as gay, which could mean that the number is closer to 25 million.

The predominance of gays in your own local population will, of course, vary depending on where you live. While South Beach Miami has been estimated to be 40 percent gay, it's a safe bet that the relative size of the gay population of Beattyville, Kentucky is considerably smaller. The 1990 Census revealed that at least 4.6 percent of all "unmarried households" in the United States (some 145,130 households) are comprised of same-sex couples. Our nation's capital has the largest proportion of same-sex couples—almost 19 percent. Wyoming has the smallest at 0.6 percent. After D.C., California, Massachusetts, New York, Minnesota, Washington, Georgia, Connecticut, Illinois, and Texas have the greatest proportions of same-sex couples. So it's true: You're not alone, even if you live in Wyoming. We *are* everywhere.

Most gay men probably vote Democratic; if not, Bill would still be Governor of Arkansas and Socks wouldn't be the cult figure he is today. The gay community should be applauded for its role in the 1992 presidential campaign, which freed us from the Dark Ages. If only Sam Nunn and a few Democratic homophobes in Congress would show their appreciation. This is not to say that there isn't a strong contingent of conservative "Log Cabin" gays. Just because a guy is gay doesn't mean he's left-wing. There are plenty of guys out there who'd rather vote for an anti-gay Republican than risk losing their tax write-offs for their leased Mercedes.

One thing is certain: People are finally beginning to recognize the political and economic clout of gay America. *The Wall Street Journal* has described the gay market as "the most potentially profitable, untapped market in the U.S. today." As a group, gay men tend to be educated, affluent, and most aren't worried about saving for junior's college tuition. The average gay male household has an income nearly 70 percent above the national average, with a considerably higher percentage of disposable income. Realizing this, a number of national catalogs, direct mail campaigns, and even mainstream retailers are now targeting the gay market. This really is the Gay Nineties.

HOTLINE: INFORMATION SOURCES FOR THE NOVICE GAY MALE

The odyssey from ostensibly straight guy to card-carrying member of the Jeff Stryker Fan Club isn't always easy, and a guy should expect a few bumps along the way. In addition to reading this book from cover to cover, here are a few suggestions to ease the transition:

1. Find the local gay hotline, and call it.

2. Find out where gay people go and when.

3. Find out where to pick up a gay newspaper, and read it.

4. Talk to a gay friend whom you respect.

5. Join a gay club, such as the Front Runners or Gay Men's Chorus.

6. Find a gay or gay-friendly doctor. (There are some things you can't even tell Mom.)

7. Volunteer at a local gay charity.

8. Rent *The Women* and commit it to memory.

An entire community is waiting to welcome the novice gay male with a wealth of information and resources. From peer counseling and AIDS information services to Parents and Friends of Lesbians and Gays (P-FLAG) and support groups for gay overeaters and other compulsives, there's a place to go or someone to talk to for just about any problem, question, or concern you might have. Don't be shy; you'd be surprised how much company you have.

Hotlines and Gay Papers in Selected Urban Areas

1. ATLANTA:

Hotline Number: (404) 892-0661
Gay Papers: *Et Cetera, Southern Voice, The News*
You can get them in: Midtown, Morningside, Virginia Highlands, Little Five Points

2. BALTIMORE:

Hotline Number: (410) 837-8888
Gay Papers: *Baltimore Gay Paper, The Alternative*
You can get them in: Mount Vernon

3. BOSTON:

Hotline Number: (617) 267-9001
Gay Papers: *Gay Community News, Bay Windows, The Guide, News Weekly*
You can get them in: Back Bay, South End

4. CHICAGO:

Hotline Number: (312) 929-HELP
Gay Papers: *Windy City Times, Chicago Outlines, Gay Chicago*
You can get them in: Lakeview, North Halsted Street

5. CLEVELAND:

Hotline Number: (216) 781-6736
Gay Paper: *Gay People's Chronicle*
You can get it in: Edgewater, Cleveland Heights, Detroit Avenue

6. DALLAS:

Hotline Numbers:	(214) 368-6283 or 528-4233
Gay Paper:	*Dallas Voice*
You can get it in:	Oaklawn, Cedar Springs Road

7. DENVER:

Hotline Number:	(303) 831-6268
Gay Papers:	*Out Front, Preferred Stock*
You can get them on:	Capitol Hill

8. DETROIT:

Hotline Number:	(313) 398-4297
Gay Papers:	*Metro Magazine, Cruise, Between the Lines* (Ann Arbor)
You can get them in:	Palmer Park

9. HOUSTON:

Hotline Number:	(713) 529-3211
Gay Papers:	*The New Voice, This Week in Texas*
You can get them in:	Montrose

10. KANSAS CITY:

Hotline Number:	(816) 931-4470
Gay Paper:	*Current News*
You can get it in:	Westport, Midtown

11. LOS ANGELES:

Hotline Number:	(213) 993-7400
Gay Papers:	*Frontiers, Edge*
You can get them in:	West Hollywood (WeHo), Silver Lake

12. MIAMI:

Hotline Number:	(305) 759-3661
Gay Papers:	*The Weekly News, The Wire, Boyz*
You can get them in:	purple boxes on street corners *(TWN)*, South Beach (SoBe)

13. MILWAUKEE:

Hotline Number:	(414) 562-7010
Gay Papers:	*Wisconsin Light, In Step Magazine*
You can get them on:	the East Side, public libraries

14. MINNEAPOLIS:

Hotline Numbers:	(612) 822-8661 or (800) 800-0907 (covers Minnesota, Wisconsin, North and South Dakota, Iowa, and Nebraska)

| | Gay Papers: | *Twin Cities GAZE, Equal Time* |
| | You can get them in: | Loring Park, Powder Hill Park |

15. NASHVILLE: Hotline Numbers: (615) 297-0008 or (800) 625-7972

Gay Paper: *Query*
You can get it in: Historic areas

16. NEW ORLEANS: Hotline Number: (504) 522-1103

Gay Papers: *Impact, Ambush, This Week Guide*

You can get them in: the French Quarter, Faubourg Marigny

17. NEW YORK: Hotline Number: (212) 777-1800

Gay Papers: *New York Native, HX, Next, OutWeek*

You can get them in: newstands in the Village, Chelsea

18. OMAHA: Hotline Number: (402) 558-5303

Gay Papers: *The New Voice, Times of the Heartland*

You can get them in: the Old Market

19. PHILADELPHIA: Hotline Number: (215) 546-7100

Gay Papers: *Philadelphia Gay News, Au Courant*

You can get them on: Spruce Street, Rittenhouse Square

20. ST. LOUIS: Hotline Number: (314) 367-0084

Gay Papers: *Lesbian and Gay News-Telegraph, Twisel*

You can get them in: Central West End

21. SAN DIEGO: Hotline Number: (619) 294-4636

Gay Paper: *Update*
You can get it in: Hillcrest, North Park

22. SAN FRANCISCO: Hotline Number: (510) 841-6224

Gay Papers: *Bay Area Reporter, San Francisco Sentinel, Bay Times*

You can get them in: the Castro, South of Market (SoMa)

23. SEATTLE: Hotline Number: (206) 443-GSBA
                 Gay Papers: *Seattle Gay News, The
                                          Guide, Twist*
                 You can get them on: Capitol Hill

24. WASHINGTON: Hotline Numbers: (202) 833-3234 or
                                          429-4971
                 Gay Paper: *The Washington Blade*
                 You can get it in: Dupont Circle, Adams
                                          Morgan

NATIONAL PUBLICATIONS OF INTEREST

1. *The Advocate*	(213) 871-1225	6922 Hollywood Blvd., 10th Fl., Los Angeles, CA 90028
2. *Genre*	(800) 576-9933	P.O. Box 25169 Anaheim, CA 92825-9908
3. *Out*	(800) 876-1199	P.O. Box 15307 North Hollywood, CA 91615-5307
4. *Out & About*	(203) 789-8518	542 Chapel Street, New Haven, CT 06511
5. *10 Percent*	(415) 905-8590	P.O. Box 885448 San Francisco, CA 94188

GOING PUBLIC:
WHEN, WHERE, HOW, AND TO WHOM

Phase I—You as the Star Attraction:
Public Appearances

Probably the first move any gay man makes in opening his closet door is to check out gay establishments. For most, that means *the gay bar.* Shocking some and tantalizing many, the gay bar has become an American institution. For the just-blossoming gay man, his first visit is a rite of passage.

Mustering the Nerve to Enter a Gay Bar, and What You'll Find There

You may not have the luxury of a gay friend to help you cross the threshold of your first gay bar. Instead, you pace back and forth outside feeling utterly ridiculous or drive around the block for what seems to be an eternity. Finally, you reluctantly venture in alone.

Upon opening the door, your worst fears are confirmed immediately: All eyes are on you (or so you think). Worst of all, everyone there knows you're gay. (It doesn't matter that they are, too.) Cowering safely in a dark corner, you catch your breath. What do you see? You've probably never studied the tops of your sneakers so intently. Eventually overcome by a blend of curiosity and adrenaline-driven excitement, you check out the place. For some, it's a fantasy come true; for others (and depending on the crowd), it can be a little frightening.

The smell: A unique blend of smoke, stale beer, and the combined bouquets of every men's cologne currently on the market. Don't worry about trying to remember the scent; your clothes will remind you of it in the morning.

The sound:
Thump, thump, thump, thump. Dance music. After a few trips to a dance club, you'll know all the latest songs. Soon you'll be starting your own collection of bootlegged DJ tapes. If a throbbing dance beat isn't your style, chances are you're listening to Barbra, Diana, k.d., or some guy at a piano bar singing "Surrey with the Fringe on Top."

The crowd:
Beneath their exteriors, they may be doctors, lawyers, truck drivers, plumbers, artists, or architects—or anything else for that matter. It's a veritable cornucopia of *man*kind. Whether it's a dance club, leather bar, or country and western corral, a trip to a gay bar instills you with a sense of community. You may be tempted to burst out in a chorus of "You'll Never Walk Alone," but unless you're in a piano bar, that's not a great idea.

Bar Strategies: Placement and Posture Tips

The key to maximizing every visit to a gay bar is knowing what image you want to project and how to project it. Do you want that "just-sauntered-in-for-a-bottled-water-on-your-way-home-from-the-gym" look? Or is the "ready, willing, and able" look more likely to get your desired results? You're sending a message whether you mean to or not. Don't let the message define you; *you* define *it*. Besides your eyes, two things—how and where you stand in the bar—tell people all you want them to know. Whether you choose the neighborhood happy hour spot, a dance club, or country and western bar, bar placement and posture are critical to master.

THE STUD

Head back, tilted slightly to the side. Leaning against a wall under a flattering spotlight (carefully selected). Arms crossed. Most importantly, a look of aloof self-satisfaction on the face. You know everyone wants you; no, wishes he <u>were</u> you. Very attractive look to some people; repels others. Works best in a town where people don't know you.

THE BROKEN WINGED BIRD

Hunched over near a wall, or in a corner, a look of thinly veiled sadness on the face, but showing courage through it all. Your lover just dumped you, and you really need someone to talk to. You're vulnerable. An emotional sitting duck. This look attracts users, so extra caution is advised when meeting people this way. Also, do you really want people's first impression to be one of pity?

THE DANCING QUEEN

Bouncing, swaying, and singing along to the music in the midst of a conversation, hips in perpetual motion. Drink in one hand, maybe a cigarette in the other. Stands near the dance floor, or creates one if none exists. Knows everyone's first name; no one's last. This is someone who likes to have a good time and has the energy for it. Great on the dance floor, though may incorporate gymnastics or modern dance into his routine. If you love to dance, like to have a good time, this is your man. Don't expect much depth, though. And whatever you do, don't crowd his spotlight.

READY, WILLING, AND ABLE

No, it's not the Three Faces of Eve. All three are there for the taking in one slinky package, strategically placed just outside the men's room door or near the exit. Knees are slightly spread (a preview of things to come?), one hand on the hip, the other in the back pocket or maybe on someone's shoulder or chest. This guy can have sex ten times a day, and often does. He's into quantity, not quality. No need for lengthy courtships with this one. The look is guaranteed to get results, but it doesn't always attract the kind of guy you'd like to take home to Mom. Or just take home, for that matter.

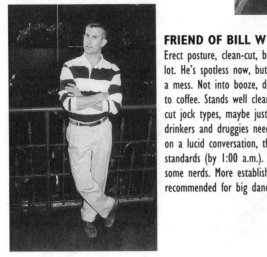

FRIEND OF BILL W

Erect posture, clean-cut, but with eyes that have seen a lot. He's spotless now, but there was a time when he was a mess. Not into booze, drugs, or cigarettes, but addicted to coffee. Stands well clear of the bar. Looking for clean-cut jock types, maybe just out of the closet. Heavy drinkers and druggies need not apply. Always able to carry on a lucid conversation, though may tire early by gay standards (by 1:00 a.m.). Attracts nice, straight-laced guys, some nerds. More established guys, too. Generally not recommended for big dance clubs or circuit parties.

THE SHY GUY

Head down, eyes focused on shoes or drink. Alone, or maybe with one shy friend. Hangs out at the end of the bar with other quiet types. Doesn't have much to say. Modest to a fault. But looks are deceiving and still waters run deep. This one's been around; that's the real reason he keeps his eyes trained down. Too many ex's. Don't be fooled. This type's shyness is a disguise. The look will attract guys looking to settle down— poor fools. He's had a million of them.

BETTY FORD DROPOUT

Slouched against the bar or the cigarette machine, a drink in one hand, another standing by, cigarette hanging out of his mouth while he speaks. The Xanax he took before leaving the house is reacting with the double martinis, and his speech is beginning to slur. An easy mark for unscrupulous types with low standards. Good sense of humor, when you can understand him. Usually travels alone, or with a small, dysfunctional group. Repels most, but attracts drug pushers and lowlifes looking for someone who won't remember them in the morning. Not pretty.

THURSTON HOWELL WANNABE

Rigid posture, starched everything, including boxer shorts. Hair short and conservative. Stands far away from the crowd, viewing the world down his nose, with a hint of disapproval. Apparently not having a good time, except in commenting on the hoi polloi around him to his cloned friend. Looking for guys with money. Willing to overlook other flaws (alcohol abuse, fitness neglect) if there's plenty of money (or at least the appearance of it). Can't dance, and wouldn't anyway. Lousy in bed (too uptight). Attracts a lot of fakes. May turn away many decent people, including some with money. Not much fun at parties.

STRANGERS IN THE NIGHT: CRUISING TECHNIQUES

Like any other art form, cruising is not something to be mastered overnight; it takes practice and is perfected only over time. There are four basic approaches:

Approach #1: Aloof Indifference

Feigned indifference is by far the most popular cruising technique. It allows the would-be suitor to look for love and deny it later if he fails. The key to this approach: *Don't look too interested.* A look of bored nonchalance can drive a guy wild. Who hasn't been on the receiving end of this one? You try desperately to catch his glance, but he continues to look right through, over, or around you. His apparent lack of interest, or failure even to know you're alive, makes your desire to be the object of his even greater.

Yet aloof indifference doesn't guarantee success. Too much indifference could leave your target totally unaware, and you could end the evening empty-handed. If you don't initially engage his interest, all that aloofness could leave you socially challenged. An occasional glance should be sufficient to sustain his interest and feed his ego just enough for him to spend the rest of the night begging for more. But if he fails to take your bait and your pride can stand it, you may want to rethink your strategy and switch to a more direct approach.

Approach #2: The Direct Hit

Believe it or not, at times honesty still is the best policy. You don't have to be an expert in geometry to know that the fastest way between two points is a straight—or rather, *direct*—line. Imagine a world where you see someone you're attracted to, and, instead of cruising him like a hawk sizing up prey, you merely walk up and introduce yourself. It's a very disarming tactic that's guaranteed to get results, though perhaps not always favorable. Those with fragile egos that can't stand rejection should consider something more subtle.

Approach #3: The Gay Stare

Versatile beyond cruising, the gay stare could tame Medusa's locks, or, with a bit of fine-tuning, turn ex-lovers into pillars of salt. The approach is simple: Lock onto the eyes of your intended like a cruise missile. (Where do you think they got the name?) Imagine your gaze boring holes right through, enabling you to see the cute blond standing behind him. Don't even *think* of blinking. If he looks down, he's afraid of what you (or he) might do if he returns the stare. If he looks to the side, he's either not interested or feigning indifference. If he returns the stare, you've got a live one, and a game of cruising "chicken" begins. You may spend the rest of the evening with both your headlights racing toward each other. Whether you go bump in the night or one of you veers off the road is up to you.

Approach #4: 1-2-3 Turn

Picture this: you're walking down the street, minding your own business, when suddenly you look up and see the man of your dreams. Be cool. Keep walking. As you pass him, start the count . . . 1-2-3, and turn. Unless he's new to the game, if he's interested, he'll turn at precisely the same moment. It's as predictable as the swallows' return to Capistrano. If you're still interested, keep walking and repeat the exercise. If he's done the same, you've hit pay dirt. Go for it.

WHERE THE BOYS ARE

New York:	8th Avenue between 14th and 23d; West Side Highway parking at Canal Street
Los Angeles:	Santa Monica Blvd., WeHo; Pavilions Grocery; Griffith Park
Chicago:	North Halsted Street; Broadway; Century Chicago Health Club
Washington:	17th Street, N.W.; P Street Beach; the Halls of Congress
Philadelphia:	Judy Garland Memorial Park; Spruce Street
Dallas:	Dallas Theater parking lot; Stevens Park Golf Course
Atlanta:	Piedmont Park
San Francisco:	The Castro; SoMa; China Beach
Austin:	Pease Park (off 24th Street)

Fine-tuning Gaydar

If there's one thing that mystifies straight people about gay men more than any other, it's their innate ability to spot another "member of the church" no matter how hard he's trying to hide it. Gaydar, the sixth sense that all gay men are born with and hone over time, is one of gay life's great gifts; and it's a good thing we've got it. With straight men finally beginning to give a damn about their appearance, now more than ever you can't judge a banana by its peel.

Interpreting that blip on your Gaydar screen may take a little practice, but in time you'll be spotting new friends all over town. Forget what's on the outside (most of all wedding rings) and focus on the eyes. A confident, knowing gaze, a look of recognition—even though you've never met—or a furtive glance lasting a split second longer than it should, all are signs that your Gaydar is up and working. Other times you *just know.*

For example: A cute guy in a college sweatshirt has his arm around some fawning female. To the untrained eye, he's hopelessly straight. But when his eyes lock onto yours, it's a direct hit. He may realize you've noticed, put up his defenses, and pull Sorority Sally closer. Give him time and trust your instincts. Eventually, you'll see him out.

"See how he's wearing a gold pinky ring, Silvia?

That is a sure give away he's gay.

If you keep at it, sooner than you think you'll get good at spotting them yourself"

GAYDAR FOR STRAIGHT PEOPLE:
How to Impress Gay Friends with Your Powers of Perception

Although straight people are Gaydar-deprived, they can learn to fake it. If any five or more of the following clues appear together in the same scenario, even Helen Keller could tell you there's family present:

highlighted hair	a baseball cap turned backwards
two men grocery shopping	group of men out, not on business
one or more earrings	a red ribbon
a good haircut	expensive sunglasses
bronzered face	moussed or gelled hair
pampered complexion	Mont Blanc or other designer pen
noticeable cologne	obvious fashion consciousness
a Village People look	carefully trimmed facial hair
tight jeans, good butt	flat stomach
gay-friendly resort T-shirt	shorts out of season
well-cared-for nails	silk ascot
pinky ring	lots of shopping bags

"Two men, one cart, fresh pasta—think about it."
—SUZANNE, FROM *DESIGNING WOMEN*, BY HARRY THOMASON AND LINDA BLOODWORTH-THOMASON

What Are These Eyes Saying?

If the eyes are the windows on the soul, gay men's eyes are picture windows. A look, after all, is worth a thousand words. The lips may lie, but the eyes seldom do. His mouth might be politely saying, "You should call me sometime," but his eyes are adding "after Hell freezes over." Test your own grasp of the language. Match these looks with their message:

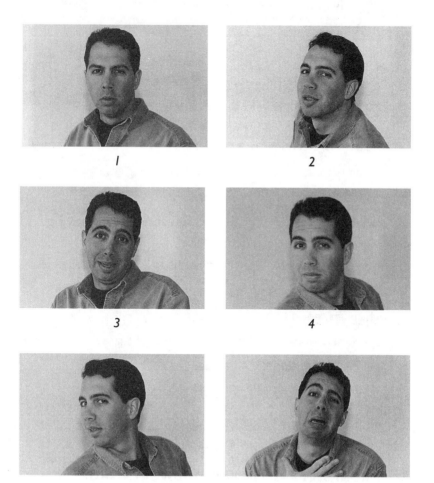

1

2

3

4

5

6

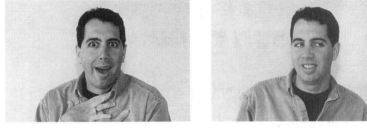

7   8

9   10

MESSAGES:

(a) Oh look, he's put on weight!

(b) He's too good-looking to be straight.

(c) I can't believe the way that slut is working it, only a week after we broke up!

(d) I'm sure that BMW is leased, just like the cute young thing he's with.

(e) I don't care how big his biceps are, I'd never go out with a man who could braid his nose hairs.

(f) I just want to be loved. Is that so wrong?

(g) Man, I look good. I could model.

(h) I wonder who they're inviting to their party.

(i) I can't believe those self-centered queens actually remembered my birthday!

(j) Enough small talk, let's go to my place.

ANSWERS:

1. (c)	2. (j)
3. (a)	4. (g)
5. (d)	6. (f)
7. (i)	8. (h)
9. (b)	10. (e)

Phase II—Your Friends:
"Some of My Best Friends Are . . ."

What Straight People Should Do When a Friend Comes Out to Them

One of the biggest problems facing many straight people when a friend or relative comes out to them is myopia. Rather than focusing on the courageous man making the revelation, their mind's eyes focus only on the impact of the news on *their* lives. For many reasons, a gay relative or friend is a benefit, not a burden. To avoid putting your foot in your mouth when a friend tells you he's gay, here are some suggestions:

1. DO congratulate him.
2. DO thank him for trusting you enough to tell you.
3. DO inquire about his lover or latest boyfriend.
4. DO invite him (or them) over with your other friends.
5. DO stay in touch.
6. DO offer to teach him to change the oil in his car in exchange for some fashion advice.
7. DO try to imagine what it would be like to be gay in a straight world.
8. DO tell him to practice safe sex.
9. DO give yourself a pat on the back for being a good friend.
10. DO give him this book.

1. DON'T treat him any differently; he's the same person he was before.
2. DON'T ask him personal questions about sex, unless you're willing to answer some yourself.
3. DON'T wonder (or ask) if he ever found you attractive.
4. DON'T think back to that time you spent the night in the same room.
5. DON'T tell anyone without his permission.

6. DON'T show him off to your friends like a rare bird.
7. DON'T offer to fix him up with the only other gay man you know—your hairdresser.
8. DON'T assume he's HIV positive.
9. DON'T tell any fag jokes.
10. DON'T be afraid to show your affection for him; he won't get the wrong idea.

"Are All the Goodlooking Men Gay?" – Relationships with Women

---

"Homosexuals make the best friends because they care about you as a woman and are not jealous. They love you but don't try to screw up your head."

—BIANCA JAGGER

Every gay man eventually realizes that his relationships with members of the opposite sex change once he's come out. The dynamics shift, and the sexual tension of Tracy & Hepburn yields to the cohorts-in-crime camaraderie of Thelma and *Louis.* Man and woman are finally able to talk to each other about really important things—like Calvin Klein's fall line. With the secure feeling that neither one is plotting to get the other into the sack, barriers are broken down.

The two eventually will trade notes on their latest sexual conquests, swap war stories about dates from hell, and advise each other on washing that man right out of their hair. When he finally meets Mr. Right, she'll be one of the first to know. But when she finds her match, their firstborn may well be on the scene before he finally gets to meet *hubby.* She's not stupid.

Unfortunately, not *every* woman responds well to the news that the man she thought was boyfriend material is just a friend. Especially if she (or worse, her *mother)* had been secretly sizing him up for a morning suit. Put yourself in her pumps for a moment: She thinks she's found the perfect man—good-looking, sensitive, nice build, and truly interested in what sweater she's wearing. Then suddenly it hits her; she realizes that his frequent flattering remarks about her outfits were fashion-consciousness, not flirting. No wonder she's spitting nails.

Aside from queens, Hell hath no fury like a woman scorned. A guy caught in this predicament may find himself the subject of a major PR campaign to salvage her image. She and her mother will save him the trouble of telling people his story. It will be like coming out on *Oprah:* "She says he only used her to hide his homosexuality." Even worse, she might dig in her heels and try to *change* him. Good luck, sister.

In most cases, after an appropriate period of sitting *shivah* and diplomatic efforts that would rival the United Nations, she'll get over it. Who knows? She may even seek his advice on bridesmaid dresses when her turn to walk down the aisle really comes. The only remaining question is . . . what's her fiancé's story?

The Curse of the Pink Wand

It's a tragic scene. A young woman gazes into the eyes of her beloved, who is cruising every guy in the joint. "Poor thing, doesn't she know?" gay men and other *cognoscenti* ask. Gay men and straight women have a lot of the same interests; it's inevitable that some poor girl won't recognize the difference between true love and a mutual fondness for Brad Pitt movies.

The first signs of the Curse of the Pink Wand—the unfortunate propensity of some women to fall *only* for gay men—usually appear in college, but sometimes are visible as early as high school. Kathleen is quite taken with Robert; he dances better than any guy on campus and always looks so put-together. Little does she know that after he drops her off at her sorority, he and a few of his fraternity brothers head out for more dancing—with each other. Sadly, upon learning the truth, Kathleen breaks it off with Robert, only to begin dating Michael, who had a fling with Robert the previous semester. Kathleen, you've got the Curse, girl. Some advice to the Kathleens of the world: If he's "not like most other guys," wake up and smell the poppers.

Phase III—Your Parents: A Captive Audience

Members of P-FLAG and other experts will tell you that timing is everything when it comes to telling parents and other family members. A basic rule: Avoid coming out to your family on holidays. The theory is that every year, parents will associate the holiday with the day they heard the Big News.

If not a holiday, when? When *you're* ready. Don't let friends or lovers push you into coming out to your family before *you* are ready to make the move. Sure, confiding in your parents and bringing them into your life—your *entire* life—can be a wonderful, liberating thing for everyone involved. But you know your relationship with your parents better than anyone. *You* decide when the time is right.

When that time comes, there are a variety of ways to break the news, from a candid conversation to a heartfelt letter . . . to writing a book like this. (Yes, Mom and Dad, it's true.) You may opt to confide in your siblings first and enlist their support. Whatever method you ultimately choose, your revelation is bound to spark more than a few questions. They will ask some but only think of others. The Rev. Merrill Proudfoot and the Sacramento P-FLAG Newsletter offered this advice:

HOW MIGHT YOU HELPFULLY RESPOND IF TOLD YOUR CHILD IS GAY?

Don't destroy any bridges that will be hard to rebuild later. Listen.

Don't reject through anger or insistence that "it's only a passing phase."

Ask questions about what you don't understand.

Avoid blaming your offspring for "living a lie all these years." You weren't told earlier because she or he didn't want to risk losing your love.

Don't try to make him or her feel guilty for making you suffer. Your child had no conscious choice of sexual orientation.

Don't suppose there is a "quick cure" available, either from a psychotherapist, a religious experience, or (worst of all!) getting married.

Don't blame yourself. Homosexuals emerge from many radically different types of environments.

Don't "bear the burden" alone. It's not a disgrace unless you make it one. Talk with your pastor, friends, other parents of gays; but respect your child's privacy by touching base with him or her about those with whom it's acceptable to share.

Read the rapidly growing body of literature, much of it for parents of gay persons.

Don't ignore the subject after that first conversation. This would not be understood as acceptance but as meaning that you can only accept your child by blotting out that part of him or her.

Get acquainted with the friends of your son or daughter. If there is a committed relationship, accept the partner as you would have accepted a spouse.

No matter how accepting your family is, your sexual orientation is not an easy topic. Their acceptance of your sexuality, like your own, isn't going to happen overnight. Be patient. Sooner or later, most parents of a gay son come to realize the joys he brings. In those increasingly rare and unfortunate cases where parents are unable to accept their son's sexuality, all is not lost; gay men provide each other with a surrogate family that may be as odd as the Addams Family, but as close as the Waltons.

Ten Things Not to Say When Telling Your Mother

The relationship between gay men and their mothers is a subject that could fill volumes, and probably does. It's been memorialized in fiction *(The Object of My Affection)*, film *(Torch Song Trilogy)*, and TV *(The Brady Bunch)*, and it's the source of endless speculation and amusement.

Despite the close bond between most gay men and their mothers, there are some things that Mom doesn't need to hear—at least not when her bundle of joy has just confided that Linda, whom he's been raving about, is really Lyle. A few things that are better left unsaid:

Ten Things Not to Say When Telling Your Mother

1. "It really doesn't hurt that much."

2. "He looks just like you."

3. "Now I know why you always hated to wear heels."

4. "It's not so bad; I could be an ax murderer."

5. "Wait till you see me do Norma Desmond!"

6. "Should I use Miss Clairol or have a professional do it?"

7. "Do you think it would hurt to have a nipple pierced?"

8. "Don't blame yourself; I think I got it from Dad."

9. "You should let me do something with that hair."

10. "Those tap lessons you made me take *really* paid off!"

Thriving in a Straight World: Are You Ready?

"I figured, as long as I had to suffer, I might as well get a tan."

—HARRY HAMLIN, IN *MAKING LOVE*

For those who think they have come to grips with it and are ready to embark on a life of whirlwind cocktail parties and countless outfit changes, a quick test:

1. You've just started at a new job, and you find yourself trapped in a conversation with your boss and others about Monday Night Football. You:
   a. pretend you're hard of hearing;
   b. suddenly remember a meeting or conference call you had;
   c. mention the name of the only pro team you know, not sure if it's even the correct sport; or
   d. try to change the subject to fashion.

2. You are driving alone in a rural area, and one of your tires goes flat. You:
   a. burst into tears;
   b. lie on the hood of your car and work on your tan, waiting for the next cute truck driver to come along;
   c. pull out your cellular phone and call the auto club for help; or
   d. walk to the nearest farmhouse and ask for assistance.

3. You're home for Thanksgiving, the guests have arrived, and your mother realizes that she forgot dessert. You:
   a. run to the store and buy a couple frozen pies;
   b. forget about dessert and scarf down extra hors d'oeuvres;
   c. ask your sister or grandmother to do something; or
   d. survey the contents of the refrigerator, give your mother a drink, and whip up something.

4. You invite some straight friends from work to a party at your home, thinking they won't accept. They do. You:
   a. cancel the party;

b. ask your gay friends to tone it down and avoid public displays of affection;

c. relax, knowing that your straight friends are adults and weren't born yesterday; or

d. invite more straight friends to try to even out the mix.

5. You are a college freshman, and the fraternity rush season begins. You:

   a. avoid fraternities like the plague;

   b. go to fraternity rush parties and stare at the attractive men;

   c. relax, be yourself, and try to find a fraternity where you feel comfortable; or

   d. wait for sorority rush season.

6. You "and Guest" are invited to a wedding. You're not dating anyone in particular, but you don't want to hang out by yourself. You:

   a. decline the invitation;

   b. bring a woman friend;

   c. bring the guy you went home with last weekend; or

   d. find out who else is invited (preferably singles) and go with them.

7. You are having lunch with work colleagues at a new restaurant. The waiter, who is attractive but has one too many earrings, calls you by your first name and asks if you had a good time the night before. You:

   a. remember the torrid evening before and turn crimson;

   b. pretend he has the wrong person;

   c. respond, "Yes, such a good time I came back for lunch and brought my colleagues from work"; or

   d. knock over your water to create a diversion.

8. You are leaving a gay bar, dressed in Spandex hot pants and Doc Martins, and you run into a group of straight friends who don't know your story. You:

   a. exclaim with surprise, "I didn't know you were gay!"

   b. duck into the nearest doorway, and hope they didn't see you;

c. tell them what a great neighborhood it is for restaurants and "progressive" clubs;

d. decide there's no time like the present to come out to them, and bring them inside to see what a gay club is like.

ANSWERS

1. *a.* *If you know what they're talking about, jump in. If not, keep your mouth shut. Just don't make a fool of yourself by trying to show off what little knowledge you have about sports. They don't call the fashion/arts/people page of the paper the "Gay Sports Section" for nothing.*

2. *c.* *If you don't know how to change a tire, learn. Those who are unwilling to learn had better buy a cellular phone or CB radio, for just this type of emergency. If you selected (a), you should see an analyst; you're gay, not helpless.*

3. *d.* *If you call yourself gay, you help out dear old mom. Would you serve frozen pies to your guests? What makes you think your mother would?*

4. *c.* *Relax and have a good time. Unless you're careless about picking friends, your straight friends should be fairly cool. If they're not, you've got to pick better friends.*

5. *c.* *Believe it or not, there are plenty of fraternities where a gay man could feel comfortable; there's no reason to exclude yourself just because you know you're "different." Some campuses even have a gay fraternity: Delta Lambda Phi. Look for the house with the manicured lawn and sumptuous window treatments.*

6. *d.* *By all means, go. Being gay doesn't mean you have to cut yourself off from all of the usual straight rituals (tired as they can sometimes be). But think twice before bringing your friend from the previous weekend, no matter how gorgeous he is. If you take him, make sure he knows which fork to use.*

7. c.   *Respond, "Yes, I had such a good time I came back for lunch and brought my colleagues from work." Your colleagues will think you'd eaten there the night before. Hope your waiter friend has enough sense to take the hint. If not, make a mental note to check the I.Q. before going out with someone new.*

8. c.   *Again, cool is the rule. Tell them what a great neighborhood it is for restaurants and "progressive" clubs. They'll think you're very hip and may even run out and buy a similar outfit.*

GAY ISN'T	GAY IS
sherbet	sorbet
minivans	convertibles
roller derby	rollerblading
Miller Lite TV ads	Miller Lite
a phase	a way of life
awesome	fabulous

CHAPTER III
PERFECTING YOUR PERSONA
Madonna Move Over

"We are all in the gutter, but some of us are looking at the stars."

—OSCAR WILDE

So you've opened the closet door, even if only enough to get a glimpse of the world that awaits you. The first thing you may notice is a sky of brilliant stars, each burning with its own individual intensity. In time, you'll probably see more than a few things your parents neglected to mention. Welcome to the universe of the gay world.

There are so many men (and so little time). Gay men are as different and diverse as the colors of the gay rainbow. They come in all types, shapes, ages, and colors. Who are they? What are they like? Most importantly, do *you* have to become just like *them?* Only if you want to.

Coming out doesn't mean you have to leave your individuality stashed away like an old leisure suit in the closet you just escaped. In the gay world you have the freedom (and acceptance) to be whatever you choose, *not* somebody else's idea of what it means to be gay. If all the world's a stage and we are merely players, don't worry: You don't have to play a role you don't like.

Guys react differently to coming out; some hardly change, others see Georgette Klinger for a total makeover. Luckily, nothing in the gay world is permanent, least of all hair color. Finding oneself is an evolution, and some guys shed personas like layers of clothes on the dance floor. Some, like chameleons, change their images with the time of day or day of the week (A-Lister lawyer by day, Club Kid by night). If a sometimes bleached blonde from Detroit can remake herself over and over and *over* again, anyone can.

Many guys find a look that works for them and perfect it, until it becomes their persona. Over time a handful of gay personas have become so refined that they've become icons of the gay world.

"If we ever get out of this, things are going to be different, I promise you. I'm going to be the man I was when we first met."
"You weren't blond then, and you wore a lot less makeup."
—JOHN RITTER AND PAM DAWBER, IN *STAY TUNED*

GAY WATCHING: A GUIDE TO THE FLORA AND FAUNA OF THE GAY WORLD

Be they simple fashion statements or a way of life, the following gay flora and fauna have been perfected with artistic precision. Even the newest student of the gay world should be able to identify them, but recognize that things are not always as they seem.

THE BIKER

Subliminal Message: "Strap your hands ' cross my engines."

Must Haves: Black leather jacket or vest, Levi's 501s, high black boots, black leather cap, ample body and facial hair, pecs, tattoos, pierced nipple, aviator sunglasses, jockstrap, chains

Accessories: Motorcycle (preferably Harley), harness, chaps, bandanna, poppers, vintage Bruce Springsteen tape

Not shown: Metallic and leather "accessories" for the bedroom, needlepoint skills, soprano voice forced to tenor

Advantages: Actually appears butch to some, scares away would-be bashers and just about everyone else, always a hit in Gay Pride Day parades

Disadvantages: Image is difficult to maintain, particularly in bed, outfits are heavy and wreak havoc at airport security checks, dog collars chafe neck

THE PIB*

Subliminal Message: "I'm too sexy for my shirt."

Must Haves: Anything in black, dark sunglasses at <u>all</u> times, vest, Italian loafers, Cartier rolling ring, Calvin Klein underwear, aloofness

Accessories: Mazda Miata, <u>faux</u> continental accent, attraction to locales with abbreviated names, such as SoBe, SoMa, SoHo, WeHo, Euro-trash friends, cross around neck, Givenchy cologne, Gitane cigarettes, ticket stubs from performance art, subscription to <u>Details</u>, Enigma CD

Not shown: Last night's tips from waiting tables, key to his room in a group house

Advantages: Unapproachable, summers at the beach (portable job skills), first one to try out new places

Disadvantages: Unapproachable, bores easily, too cool for most people, jobs, and places, eye strain

*Person in Black

THE CLUB KID

Subliminal Message: "Where's the party?"

Must Haves: Pussy pants, tear-away top, chains, heavy white socks, Doc Martins, baseball cap (turned backwards), tattoo (temporary), multiple-pierced ear, dancing agility

Accessories: Wearable objets d'art, cab fare, Walkman, fanny pack, adept use of slang, Ecstasy, Special K, et al. (in sock), gum, directions to morning party, bootlegged DJ tape

Not shown: Eviction notice, familiarity with artist, title, and beats per minute of all current dance hits

Advantages: Young (or thinks he is), no responsibilities, knows every bouncer and bartender in town

Disadvantages: Always looks tired, pants ride up, often loses ID (no pockets), out of place anywhere but the gay ghetto, somewhat unemployable

THE OPERA QUEEN

Subliminal Message: "Sempre avanti!"

Must Haves: Black evening wear, silk scarf, gold ring, affected urbane accent, encyclopedic knowledge of major operas

Accessories: Mercedes (often leased), season tickets to opera, symphony, and ballet (purchased or comp'd), pocket square, full figure, exaggerated gestures, well-fed tabby, Brie and D.P., subscriptions to Connoisseur and Opera News, The Ring Cycle LPs

Not shown: Familiarity with Italian, German, and French phrases and frequent (sometimes inappropriate) use of them, references to opera divas by single name, contributions to arts and AIDS organizations

Advantages: Broader horizons, wholesome alternative to bar scene, often invited to swank cocktail parties

Disadvantages: Conversational skills require knowledge of arcane opera plots, unfamiliar with contemporary culture, interests are expensive to indulge

THE ACTIVIST

Subliminal Message: "The Cause is my life."

Must Haves: Unwashed T-shirt with logo or slogan of cause <u>du jour</u>, buttons with vehement statements, baggy jeans, black socks, black boots or beat-up black gym shoes, goatee, pierced ear, nose, lip, eyebrow, or other body part, handmade jewelry, beret, determination

Accessories: Bus ticket, tattoo, spray paint, posters and tape, leaflets, condoms (for handing out), handcuffs (for attaching self to fences), coffee, tattered copy of <u>OutWeek</u>, stray kitten, Sinead O'Conner cassette

Not shown: Arrest record, keys to book or record store, self-righteousness, ticket stub from gay film festival, disdain for "straight-acting" gays

Advantages: Always politically correct, self-satisfaction, lots of press coverage

Disadvantages: Always politically correct, sometimes criticized for working outside, rather than inside, the system, difficult to integrate persona with mainstream career

A ROSE BY ANY OTHER NAME: TAKING A GAY NAME

There are certain names that gay men just seem to gravitate toward, or vice versa. Has anyone ever met a straight Justin? Or, in naming a baby boy Bruce, are his proud parents predetermining his sexuality or merely anticipating it? Why is it that for every straight Tom, Dick, and Harry, there's a gay Thomas, Richard, and Harold? For some reason, many gay men seem to feel that their names are too ordinary. If you're one of them, consider making your name more en*gay*ing, like so:

Bob becomes Robert
Steve becomes Stephen
Mike becomes Michael
Jeff becomes *Geoffrey*
Bruce becomes J.T., Skip, Chip, or *anything* else for that matter.

THE POODLE

Subliminal Message: "Only my hairdresser knows for sure."

Must Haves: Gold, gold, and <u>more</u> gold, oversized silk shirt, tropical weight wool pants with generous pleats, Cartier-look watch, diamond pinky ring, pearls, knock-off Gucci loafers, bikini briefs, Armani eyewear

Accessories: Jaguar or Jaguar keychain, Neiman Marcus charge card, Chanel No. 5, eyelash curler, gift certificate to Georgette Klinger, Bichon or Shih Tzu puppy, martini glass, Korbel, carton of Virginia Slims, subscriptions to <u>Metropolitan Home</u> and <u>Women's Wear Daily</u>, <u>Phantom of the Opera</u> CD

Not shown: Scars from facelift, tanning salon membership, hangover, dark roots, key to his design studio, date of birth

Advantages: Knows the best manicurist in town, a hit with wealthy old ladies, often serving as a walker, incredible staying power

Disadvantages: CFCs in hairspray deplete ozone layer, insurance for jewelry expensive, limited career possibilities (being somewhere before 10:00 a.m. is <u>simply</u> out of the question)

THE A-LISTER

Subliminal Message: "I come from money."

Must Haves: Polo shirt (sometimes worn over white T-shirt), khaki shorts or trousers, boxers, deck shoes (never worn on a boat) or assorted L. L. Bean footwear, no socks, belt with nautical motif, Rolex, Ray-Bans, Attitude

Accessories: BMW or Mercedes (often leased), his own place, signet or Ivy League class ring, tuxedo, revisionist family history, WASP name (real or assumed), year-round tan, golden retriever or yellow lab, Gold Amex, subscription to <u>Town & Country</u>, bottled water, anything with names of tony resorts, Frank Sinatra albums

Not shown: Diploma from State College, debt, <u>Preppy Handbook</u>

Advantages: Highly employable, wardrobe never goes out of style

Disadvantages: Thinks he passes for straight, calluses from social climbing, bronzer stains shirt collars

> "Being an A-Gay means never having to say you're an old troll . . . Just look at those ancient A-Gays wandering around Sutton Place. Like gargoyles on top of Notre Dame cathedral—ugly as hell, but very difficult to knock off."
>
> —T. R. WITOMSKI, IN *KVETCH*

THE BOHEMIAN

Subliminal Message: "Think globally, act locally."

Must Haves: Nothing. Old flannel shirt, secondhand trousers or overalls, worn sandals or hiking boots, bandanna (worn like a migrant worker), earring, antique wire-rim glasses, three-day-old beard, familiarity with obscure literature

Accessories: 1967 VW Bug with Greenpeace bumper sticker, Granola, macramé plant hangers, recycling bin, guitar, mantra, back issues of <u>Mother Jones</u>, Grateful Dead albums

Not shown: Erratic personal hygiene, reverse snobbism, key to efficiency in Haight-Ashbury, Adams Morgan, or the East Village, paystub from plant shop or Ben & Jerry's, fondness for foreign films

Advantages: Good nutrition, inexpensive habits, environmentally friendly

Disadvantages: Should have been born Amish, hard to shop for

THE BOY NEXT DOOR

Subliminal Message: "Gee whiz."

Must Haves: Jean jacket, college sweatshirt, jeans, jockey briefs, fraternity pin, Timex watch, tennis shoes

Accessories: Nissan Stanza with ski rack, Smithsonian membership, tennis racket (he actually plays), Miller Lite, subscription to <u>Newsweek</u>, Whitney Houston cassette

Not shown: Condo in the burbs, recipe for mother's meatloaf, high school yearbook, Midwestern accent, incredible sex life, savings account

Advantages: Timeless, all-American, probably working in the office next door, simple tastes, can talk sports with Dad, Mom will be pleased

Disadvantages: Most likely to attract women

THE COWBOY

Subliminal Message: "Ride 'em, cowboy."

Must Haves: Stetson, mustache, longjohns with rear flap, heavy corduroy or flannel shirt, bolo tie or neckerchief, leather vest, worn jeans, wide leather belt with silver belt buckle, Tony Lammas boots

Accessories: Chevy pickup, ticket stubs from Gay Rodeo, knowledge of the Texas two- and three-step, Marlboros, Lone Star beer, coiled rope, Tammy Wynette and k.d. lang tapes

Not shown: Brooklyn accent, bonsai hobby, bridge club membership

Advantages: Butch look, travels well in Southern and Western states, opportunities to socialize with <u>real</u> cowboys

Disadvantages: Blisters from boots worn only on weekends, often asked for advice on car repairs, attracts NRA types

THE CLONE

Subliminal Message: "Pride."

Must Haves: Close-cropped hair, trimmed mustache and/or beard, tank top (warm weather) or flannel shirt, with or without sleeves (cold weather), Levi's jeans (regular length or cut-off), heavy socks, construction boots

Accessories: Subway token, color-coded handkerchief strategically placed in left or right back pocket, pierced ear, Budweiser, subscription to <u>The Advocate</u>, worn-out Donna Summer album from late '70s

Not shown: Key to apartment in the Castro or the West Village, worn membership card to now-closed baths, joint

Advantages: Remembers Stonewall, comprehensive knowledge of gay lore, not concerned with leading double life, wardrobe inexpensive

Disadvantages: Look invites redneck reaction, sees himself coming and going

---

"I get tired of hearing the pissing and moaning about clones. Because people who choose to wear clone costumes are choosing to be publicly homosexual. I think that's a political act itself. I would endorse them over any coat-and-tie faggot any day of the week."

—ARMISTEAD MAUPIN

THE SUGAR DADDY
Subliminal Message: "Money <u>can</u> buy me love."
Must Haves: Money
Accessories: White or gray hair, perma-tan, facial lines from years of overexposure to sun, loud (often madras) pants, gold jewelry, Lagerfeld cologne, Bally shoes, Eldorado or Mercedes, large home, valuable antiques, mother's china, subscriptions to <u>Travel & Leisure</u> and <u>Architectural Digest</u>, Tanqueray & tonic, Barbra and Liza CDs
Not shown: String of young, good-looking boyfriends, lasciviousness, ability to name-drop with flair, skeletons in the closet
Advantages: Younger men, purse strings, fawning attention from restaurateurs, florists, and designers
Disadvantages: Expensive

THE GYM DANDY
Subliminal Message: "Look, but don't touch."
Must Haves: Anything formfitting in Lycra, tank top, razor or other hair remover, gym membership and gym bag, weight belt and gloves, sweat socks, Reebok cross trainers, mirror
Accessories: Honda with bike rack, weights, Gatorade, Power Bars, mountain bike, sports watch, vitamins, subscription to <u>Men's Fitness</u>, aerobics tapes
Not shown: Steroids, chemically highlighted hair, self-tanning lotion, pathological desire to take shirt off in public, recipes for fat-free tuna, pasta, and chicken dishes
Advantages: Great body, inexpensive wardrobe
Disadvantages: Weak conversational skills (muscles deny blood to brain), trouble dating (too focused on own body), looks awkward in most street clothes

UNITED WE STAND: GAY TYPES BY CITY

Like it or not, every town has a stereotype in the eyes of out-of-towners. It is said, for instance, that New Yorkers think New York is the center of the universe—no, New York *is* the universe. Gays in our Nation's Capital are often said to be starched walking résumés. And L.A. boys are frequently characterized by the "three Bs"—blond, bronzed, and built. We've polled scores of gay men across the country, and here's how they view their compatriots in other cities:

1. NEW YORK: Urbane, tending toward decadent, believing that New York is the Mother of All Cities. Lots of lawyers, bankers, and people in vaguely defined artsy careers wearing never-before-seen fashions. Motto: "Seen it, done it, had him."

2. LOS ANGELES: Blond and built, but bimbos. Actor/model/waiters. More gyms in L.A. than libraries. Motto: "Enough about me; what do *you* think about me?"

3. CHICAGO: Corn-fed all-American boys, big, earnest, and drawn to the gay mecca of the Midwest. Loyal friends. A few months behind the latest fad, but could care less. Motto: "I can't wait for you to meet Mom."

4. DALLAS: Beefy, bow-legged, beer-drinking cowboys dressed in Brooks Brothers' best. Smooth-talking Texans who could charm the pants right off you. They may be in petroleum products, but not necessarily the kind J. R. Ewing coveted. Motto: *"Everything* in Texas is BIG."

67

5. WASHINGTON: Career- and status-obsessed clean-cut guys networking their way up the ladder. More button-downs than a Lands' End catalog, more lawyers than even New York, boring in bed. Motto: "I was dining with the President last night and . . ."

6. MIAMI: Tanned Cuban beauties in extravagant Versace outfits. Aspiring models working as waiters by day and go-go dancers by night. Motto: "Oh my God! I've got a hang-nail!"

7. PHILADELPHIA: Muscled Italian men in tight white T-shirts and even tighter jeans. Blue-collar workers or at least blue-collar taste. South Jersey accents. Motto: "Yo!"

8. ATLANTA: Frat boys turned Southern belles. Dressed in madras or Day-Glo pants, often with whale or pheasant embroidery. Good ol' boys who work for their fathers and keep some unsuspecting woman in tow for charity balls. Motto: "Tomorrow is another day."

9. SAN FRANCISCO: Men to be admired. They've stared Hell in the face and lived to tell. More leather and Levi's than in the Lone Star State. Clones that are almost anachronistic in the '90s. Motto: "Pride."

10. MINNEAPOLIS: Tall, blond, strapping Swedes. Even more homespun than the men of Chicago. Executives in agribusiness or Northwest flight attendants. Lots of great sweaters. Motto: "Skoal!"

11. SEATTLE: Moss enthusiasts enjoying stable-relationship bliss or grunge lumberjack types with correct social consciences. With more cappuccino counters than slugs on the sidewalk, there's good reason guys are sleepless. Motto: "We like it wet."

12. SALT LAKE CITY: Adventurous men of pioneer stock and the lost pink sheep of the Mormon flock gathering at alternative temples where a joyous chorus is heard. Motto: "Come West, young men."

NEARER MY GOD TO THEE: GAYS AND RELIGION

Despite the claims of some, gay men aren't the heretical descendants of Sodom and Gomorrah. (In fact, history has given Sodom and Gomorrah a bum rap. Some scripture suggests that they weren't destroyed for sodomy but for enjoying much of the good life but failing to be charitable with their wealth. Luke 10:10–12, Ezekiel 16:49–50. While the former may be true of many modern gay men, the latter is certainly not.)

As might be expected, some of the loudest voices in the church choir and most prolific producers at church bake sales often are the gay men in the congregation. Cynics might say that gays' attraction to religion is understandable, what with the pomp and circumstance, the music, and all the blue hairs in furs. But when it comes to a relationship with that higher being, what could possibly make a gay man different from anyone else? Absolutely nothing. Sorry, Pat Robertson. Gay Jews have caught on; one of their prominent religious organizations is Bet Mishpachah, which means "House of the Family." For gay Catholics, it's a simple matter of Dignity.

Like so many other decisions we face in life, religion, be it institutional or individual, is a matter of personal choice. If one decides to go the more traditional route, the key is to select a church or synagogue carefully. For those who don't know where to begin searching for the right religious group, there are several gay religious organizations. Besides Dignity and Bet Mishpachah, Episcopalians have Integrity, Methodists and Mormons each have their own Affirmation; and there are Presbyterians for Lesbian/Gay Concerns, Lutherans Concerned, Evangelicals Concerned, and the Unitarian Lesbian/Gay Caucus. The Metropolitan Community Church, an independent Christian organization, is a popular choice. The point is, if you're gay and you want religion, it's out there. Seek and ye shall find.

IT WASN'T ONLY THE NINETIES THAT WERE GAY: ROLE MODELS IN HISTORY

Gays have contributed a lot more to history than great hairstyles. For instance, it's been said that gays undoubtedly launched the Renaissance when they hatched the notion of painting portraits of husky, naked men in biblical settings. Before that, the ancient Greeks not only accepted but celebrated gay love. Plato, for example, in his fourth century B.C. *Symposium,* praised a prominent gay couple of the time:

> The man whom the gods honored above all was Achilles, the son of Thetis. They sent him to the Islands of the Blessed . . . Out of loyalty to his lover Patroclus he chose without hesitation to die—not to save him, but to avenge him; for Patroclus had already been killed. The gods were full of admiration, and gave him the highest possible honor, because he valued his lover so highly.

Plato's just one of many well-known historical figures who was gay. Some of the better known of our other gay predecessors include:

Alexander the Great (born 356 B.C.). King of Macedon and conqueror of most of Asia, a military genius. Also one of history's most vindictive queens. When a physician failed to save the life of Alexander's lover, Alexander had him crucified; when a high government official derided a eunuch lover of Alexander's, the official was put to death.

Gaius Julius Caesar (born 100 B.C.). Roman emperor whose image was damaged when the public learned that he was the bottom to the King of Bithynia's top, as reported by Cicero, the Truman Capote of his time. (When the King died, he left his kingdom to Rome.) Although considered inappropriate for all but adolescent boys during Caesar's time, the fashion later changed, leading one anonymous writer to remark that "Roma, which delighted in making love from behind, spelled 'Amor'—love—by inverting its own name."

The Emperor Hadrian (born A.D. 76). Roman emperor whose gorgeous lover, Antinoüs, reportedly drowned himself at twenty-one rather than age and lose his looks. We've all been there. Hadrian spent a fortune building a city of the same name to commemorate the lad.

Richard the Lion-Hearted (born 1157). King of England honored by history for his military prowess and chivalry. Had a documented love affair with Philip, King of France, when he was Duke of Aquitaine. A real power couple. Although he later married, he fathered no children. His marriage was not even recognized by the Church until after his death, when his widow had to sue the Pope to be recognized as the King's widow.

 **Edward II** (born 1284). King of England who, though married, had two longtime male companions, Piers Gaveston and Hugh le Despenser. The latter was castrated and beheaded for being gay; Edward was killed by having a red-hot poker shoved up his rear. Don't try this at home.

Leonardo da Vinci (born 1452). Italian inventor, painter, true Renaissance man, who pioneered gay networking, reportedly hiring his assistants for their looks. Homophobic critics have charged that his "Mona Lisa" is really a man in drag. Bad drag. Left his estate to his two male assistants.

Michelangelo Buonarroti (born 1475). Italian sculptor, painter who was outed centuries later in "Dear Abby." In addition to the David, the Pietà, and the Sistine Chapel, his works include love sonnets to his lover, Tommaso Cavalieri.

William Shakespeare (born 1564). Playwright, poet who wrote sonnets to a man he called the "master-mistress of [his] passion." Although Shakespeare's proclivities are subject to heated debate, could a straight man have written *A Midsummer Night's Dream*?

Voltaire (born 1694). French writer thought to have had a love-hate relationship with Frederick the Great. He wrote that sodomy, when not accompanied by violence, should not be illegal. Nevertheless, when a friend asked about trying gay sex a second time, Voltaire is said to have remarked, "Once a philosopher, twice a sodomite!"

Frederick the Great (born 1712). King of Prussia. As a young man, he ran away with his lover, Hans von Katte, only to be caught by his disapproving father, who put the lover to death. Wrote gay love songs at his glam palace, Sans-Souci.

Alexander Hamilton (born 1755). First Secretary of the Treasury, who is rumored to have been more than just compatriots with George Washington, and who wrote love letters to a certain John Laurens, saying in one, "I wish, my dear Laurens, it might be in my power, by action rather than words, [to] convince you that I love you." How touching.

James Buchanan (born 1791). Fifteenth President of the United States, and the only bachelor in the White House. His twenty-year roommate was Senator William Rufus DeVane King, whom Andrew Jackson and writers of the time called "Miss Nancy" or "Aunt Fancy."

Hans Christian Andersen (born 1805). Danish writer of fairy tales, in the truest sense of the word. Wanted to be a seamstress (tailor), then an opera singer, wound up being supported by an older poet while he penned his tales, some of the earliest examples of high camp.

Herman Melville (born 1819). American writer whose works included *Billy Budd* (the "Beautiful Sailor") and *Moby-Dick* (in which two male characters, Ishmael and Queequeg, jump in bed together). Melville was infatuated with straight, unreciprocating Nathaniel Hawthorne. Reviewing Hawthorne's book *Mosses from an Old Manse,* Melville wrote, "Already I felt that this Hawthorne has dropped germinous seeds into my soul. He expands and deepens down, the more I contemplate him; and further and further, shoots his strong New England roots into the hot soil of my Southern soul." Take a cold shower, Herman.

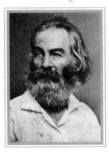

Walt Whitman (born 1819). American poet who gave us "I Sing the Body Electric." In "When I Heard at the Close of Day," Walt wrote that his happiest moment was when "the one I love most lay sleeping by me under the same cover in the cool night . . . And his arm lay lightly around my breast—and that night I was happy."

Horatio Alger, Jr. (born 1832). One-time Unitarian minister-turned-author known for his books for young men. His interest in boys got him expelled from his hometown of Brewster, Massachusetts. When he arrived in New York, he "informally adopted" several young men. His first book was *Ragged Dick.*

Peter Ilyich Tchaikovsky (born 1840). Composer of *The Nutcracker,* among other masterpieces. Who but a gay man could write "Dance of the Sugar Plum Fairy"? Although he reluctantly married, his lack of enthusiasm for his wife led her first to have an affair and then to be institutionalized.

Oscar Wilde (born 1854). Irish writer and martyr to the cause. He was imprisoned for sodomy. Called by one writer the "patron saint of the one-liner," Wilde is notable as much for his offhand remarks as for his writing. Not one to adhere to others' standards of conduct, he once said, "Morality is simply the attitude we adopt toward people whom we personally dislike."

Sigmund Freud (born 1856). German psychologist whose lover was Berlin physician Wilhelm Fliess. Query whether the term "Freudian slip" originally referred to lingerie or to something that happened in the shower.

Winston Churchill (born 1874). Although clearly not exclusively gay, when asked by W. Somerset Maugham whether it were true that he had affairs with men in his youth, Churchill reportedly responded, "Not true! But I once went to bed with a man to see what it was like." When Maugham asked how it was, Churchill is said to have answered, "Musical."

W. Somerset Maugham (born 1874). British playwright, novelist, short story writer. He reportedly said that his biggest mistake was that "I was a quarter normal and three quarters queer, but I tried to persuade myself it was the other way round."

Cole Porter (born 1891). One of America's greatest native songwriters. His songs, with titles such as "My Heart Belongs to Daddy," occasionally gave him away: "But if, baby, I'm the bottom, you're the top!"

J. Edgar Hoover (born 1895). Director of the FBI and part-time cross-dresser. Had a companion, Clyde Tolson, for forty-four years. In spite of this achievement, Hoover was a little weird, and he's not someone we brag about.

Rudolph Valentino (born 1895). The reportedly "gifted" film star and Casanova wrote in his journal that "A very good-looking boy followed me for a quarter of an hour, and in the end he came up to me outside the Opera . . . I went back with him to his home . . . I was wildly passionate . . . We made love like tigers until dawn." Red Rover, Red Rover, send Rudy right over.

Tennessee Williams (born 1911). Playwright whose *A Streetcar Named Desire, The Glass Menagerie, Cat on a Hot Tin Roof,* and *Suddenly Last Summer* are classics. Credited as being the first "openly gay" American celebrity, he wrote in his memoirs, "I have had a remarkably fortunate life which has contained a great many moments of joy, both pure and impure."

William S. Burroughs (born 1914). Author and heir to the Burroughs Adding Machine Company fortune. Bisexual and tragic, he accidentally killed his wife when he was playing William Tell and tried to shoot a champagne glass off her head. The glass survived.

James Baldwin (born 1924). African-American author of *Go Tell It On the Mountain,* among other landmark works. His 1956 novel, *Giovanni's Room,* was about gay love and became a metaphor for the proverbial closet. An excellent Philadelphia gay bookstore borrowed the title for its name.

Gore Vidal (born 1925). Writer whose works include the novels *The City and the Pillar,* the candid story of a gay man, and *Myra Breckenridge,* the story of a transsexual, and the screenplay for *Ben-Hur.* When asked whether the first person he slept with was a man or a woman, Vidal reportedly responded, "I don't know; I was too polite to ask."

Edward Albee (born 1928). American playwright whose acclaimed *Who's Afraid of Virginia Woolf?,* depicting a dysfunctional marriage, was said by some critics to portray gay relationships, with the female characters really men in drag. And you thought it was just Liz Taylor in a cheap wig.

David Kopay (born 1942). Running back for the San Francisco Forty-Niners, Detroit Lions, Washington Redskins, New Orleans Saints, and Green Bay Packers. The first pro athlete to come out voluntarily. If only the many others would open their locker doors.

GAY OR QUEER?

As if life's not complicated enough, now we have to decide whether we're "queer" or "gay." Not an easy choice. On the one hand, the term "gay" has come to refer primarily to men, while "lesbian" of course means women; "queer" is gender-neutral and therefore some find it preferable. On the other hand, some believe that "queer" has derogatory overtones and buys into all the B.S. the world's homophobes have been shouting for centuries. But proponents of "queer" argue that that's exactly the point: By taking a term that others have used to oppress gays, we're saying, "Sticks and stones may break our bones, but names will never hurt us." The bottom line is that, gay or queer, we're talking about the same group. Gays/Queers have too many *important* issues to fight for (like equal rights) to waste time arguing over nomenclature. Dividing the ranks won't further the cause.

THE GAY NATIONAL PASTIME: SHOPPING

"I told her you spoke two languages. She said yes, English and Gucci."

—RON SILVER, IN *GARBO TALKS*

Gay men are inveterate shoppers. They've made the search for just the right tie a competitive sport that requires years of training and piles of credit card statements. Visit the shopping meccas of the world—Rodeo Drive, Worth Avenue, or Fifth Avenue, to name a few—and whom do you find? Every Thomas, Richard, and Harold in town, browsing through the latest in everything from sweaters to swimwear. The same scene is repeated in malls throughout the country. The spending habits of gay men have undoubtedly saved many a retailer from insolvency.

Gay men have many looks, but they all share an obvious attention to detail. For those who are looking to make themselves over and don't know where to begin, some highlights in retail:

All American Boy   *New York, San Francisco, West Hollywood, Fire Island.*
For the gay look *du jour,* this is the place. A chain with real staying power.

Barneys   *7th Avenue at 17th, and Madison at 61st, New York.*
Perhaps the world's leading men's clothing store, with a huge variety of clothes as well as prices. You can spend a fortune if you want, but you can also find some bargains. A day at Barneys is worth making a trip to New York.

The Boy Next Door   *Piedmont Road, Atlanta.*
Club wear and workout gear. Hot looks not for every body.

Boyds   *18th & Chestnut, Center City, Philadelphia.*
Suits and work clothes for the fashion-conscious professional.

Britches of Georgetown   *metropolitan Washington, D.C.*
Where Washington's walking résumés shop for business clothes. Conservative clothing with some flair. Moderately expensive.

Cignal   *Century Mall, Chicago, and other tony malls throughout the country.*
For aspiring Persons in Black, everything you'll need to create that way-cool look except the attitude.

Enertia Sport   *15th & Walnut, Center City, Philadelphia.*
Workout clothes for those who can carry them off, or think they can.

Fred Siegel   *Melrose Avenue, West Hollywood.*
Huge variety of cool clothes, from grunge to business wear by every hip designer under the sun. Be prepared: Like the clothes, the prices are out of this world.

The Gap   *Virtually everywhere.*
If you're looking to create the Boy-Next-Door look, this is your place. Good clothes at reasonable prices. Selection sometimes is a bit monochromatic, but it's generally a winner.

Hugo Boss   *New York and other major cities.*
Stylish clothes that look a bit out of place in conservative employment environs, but a bonanza for those with a bit more imagination.

International Male   *Santa Monica Boulevard, West Hollywood.*
It's not just a catalog. You can actually browse through the show-

room in the middle of L.A.'s gay ghetto, but can you see yourself in any of the clothes?

Neiman Marcus *Dallas and nationwide.*
"Needless Markup." Expensive department store for those with an oil well in their backyard.

Off Gear *17th Street, N.W., Washington, D.C.*
Club wear, casual sports clothes, and workout clothes; accessories and grooming products. Gay owned, good selection, and conveniently located near some favorite watering holes.

Patricia Field *8th Street between 5th and University, New York.*
Everything a drag queen could desire. Home of the respected House of Field, and reputed former employer of Queen Bee Ru-Paul. You better shop!

The Polo "Mansion" *Madison at 61st, New York.*
De rigueur traditional clothes for would-be A-Listers striving for that old-money look. You can make your whole life Polo, with linens, china, flatware, draperies, and more. Swell. For more athletic types, check out Polo Sport, across the street.

Rock Creek *P Street, N.W., Washington, D.C.*
Workout clothes and casual sportswear for a masculine look. Gay owned with very friendly staff. Highly recommended.

Rolo *Castro Street, San Francisco.*
Casual wear with a bit of grunge flair, great looks for guys under thirty.

Sporting Club *Santa Monica Boulevard, West Hollywood.*
Purveyors of the West Hollywood uniform: hot gym wear and great T-shirts.

Tommy at the Beach *Ocean Drive, South Beach, Miami.*
Club wear: kilts, pussy pants, and accessories for the quintessential Miami look, whether you're there for the season or just a long weekend. Its more butch sister, Tommy Sport, is across the street.

"Are you unhappy because you didn't get to wear my dress?"
"If I had worn your dress it would have hung properly."
—MAGGIE SMITH AND MICHAEL CAINE, IN
CALIFORNIA SUITE

Let Your Fingers Do the Walking: Catalog Shopping

Okay, so you don't live in Metropolis and you may not be able to get there to shop for your fall wardrobe. Fear not: The days of buying your evening wear at Sears are over. Now every gay man is just a 1-800 number away from wearing the same studded vest seen on the bronzed backs of would-be (porn) stars posing at Hollywood and Vine. (But would it play in Peoria?) Thanks to mail order catalogs such as International Male, no matter where a gay man lives, he can enjoy the latest in athletic supporters in a variety of fashion colors without those unsightly leg straps. Or if he's looking for that relaxed, almost wrinkled Nantucket-in-Autumn look, but lives in El Paso, no problem—J. Crew ships just about anywhere.

"Take your average straight lawyer from Des Moines, who's married with three kids—his taste is terrible. Take a gay lawyer in the same city, and he'll look a lot better."

—EGON VON FURSTENBERG

SOME MAIL ORDER FAVORITES

International Male—For some, the *Women's Wear Daily* of gay fashion. Hunky guys in some of the most progressive (or aggressive) clothing available, sporting more skin than fabric. Even if you can't imagine wearing anything from its pages, the models are worth a look at the catalog. To order, call 800-293-9333 (hearing impaired persons can use TDD at 800-972-5280).

J. Crew—A classic American mail order sensation that has prompted straight and gay men alike to rush to their phones, further blurring the line between the two. Why does everyone want to look like a young George (or Barbara) Bush on the beach in Kennebunkport? To order, call 800-782-8244.

Lands' End—A pioneer in the Econo-preppy-by-mail business, it's out of touch with the tastes of most gay men and just about everyone else who doesn't live in Wisconsin. Still, you can't beat it for no-nonsense, no-frills clothes. To order, call 800-356-4444 (800-541-3459 for hearing impaired persons).

L.L. Bean—A particular favorite of Bohemians (and A-Listers striving for the duck hunter look). After years of not using models, it has finally realized that the clothes aren't the only reason you check out a catalog. To order, call 800-221-4221 (800-545-0090 for hearing impaired persons).

Made in Gay America—Fun casual wear for the active gay man. A great assortment of humorous "Don't Panic" and other T-shirts that have become a hallmark of the new gay sensibility. When it comes time to pay your bill, write a check on one of theirs, displaying a pink triangle or red ribbon. To order, call 800-USA-GAYS (800-872-4297).

Shocking Gray—Everything for the politically correct gay man (and woman). Where else could you find little statues of two men to top off a wedding cake? Or a windbreaker (or dog collar) sporting the rainbow colors of the gay flag? Call 800-788-4729.

Undergear—Like its female counterpart, *Victoria's Secret,* it's borderline soft porn. The photos bring hours of pleasure, but you'd better have a body of death (or a lot of self-esteem) to actually order anything. Call 800-853-8555 (hearing impaired TDD 800-972-5280).

LOOKING GOOD ON (NOT IN) A SHOESTRING— LIVING WITHIN YOUR MEANS

"Remember, my people, there is no shame in being poor . . . only [in] dressing poorly."
—GEORGE HAMILTON, IN ZORRO, THE GAY BLADE

One of the greatest dilemmas facing many gay men is that money seems to go out faster than it comes in. Oh, cruel world. For the truly fashion-conscious, deficit spending can eventually be devastating. If left unchecked, a guy's love affair with VISA, MasterCard, and Amex can turn sour. For those familiar with this feeling, a few tips for building up your wardrobe *and* your self-restraint:

1. If you can only see yourself in an item if a chain of improbable events occurs (e.g., you take up sailing, travel to Newport, and are invited to compete in the America's Cup), put it down and come back to earth.

2. There's a reason those svelte guys in the magazines look good in the clothes they're wearing: They're *paid* to look good. Before buying that form-fitting Del-Mar bathing suit, compare your physique with the golden god modeling it (who, by the way, spends five hours a day at the gym). Maybe you should consider baggy surfer jams.

3. Don't buy into the "You-Can't-Imagine-What-I-Paid-for-This-Outfit" game. You don't have to spend a lot of money to look good. A white T-shirt and well-fitting pair of jeans are still the hottest ensemble.

4. Some of the biggest fashion *faux pas* and frivolous spending occur when gay men venture too far afield from their usual looks. Picture the fortyish accountant who clearly would be more comfortable in a button-down and khakis, but finds himself poured into some skimpy disco bunny getup. He's a *Glamour* Don't if there ever was one. Make the most of *your* look; don't try to make something of someone else's.

THE GAY MAN'S PURSE: THE GYM BAG

Some guys don't feel funny carrying a handbag, and opt for one of those little leather "clutches" for men. These guys are either very comfortable with their own masculinity or don't give a damn about it. Those not ready or willing to make the bold fashion statement of car-

rying a tasteful Chanel knockoff make do with a butch gym bag, bearing the logo of their favorite workout spot or university. (Tommy Hilfiger bags are also big, though considerably less butch.) The contents of these gym bags vary, of course, but some constants likely to be found in most are:

—keys

—address book

—checkbook

—scraps of paper with names and phone numbers

—Binaca (sugarless)

—extra outfit for later

—street shoes

—condoms

—lock

—blowdryer

—wallet

—Walkman

—tapes

—towel

—brush

—favorite grooming products—shampoo, conditioner, deodorant, powder, bronzer, gel or mousse, cologne

—$1.25 in quarters and assorted loose change (for parking meters and pay phones)

—workout diary

—weight belt (if really serious)

—weight gloves (whether serious or not)

—cross training or aerobics shoes

—oh yeah, and gym clothes

GROOMING

"What color is this? I ask for a simple rinse, and that ditzy queen's given me crayon."
—MAGGIE SMITH, IN *CALIFORNIA SUITE*

Gay men are the *last* people on earth who need grooming tips. Still, no one's perfect, and there are just a few areas in which even gay men sometimes get careless. Some reminders:

1. Avoid mousse abuse. It attracts bugs and, with a spark, could transform your coif into a Roman candle. Don't be known *literally* as a flaming queen.

2. Go easy with the cologne. Its environmental impact is only beginning to be understood. And nothing can ruin an evening like asphyxiating a date with your Eternity for Men.

3. If you must color your hair, have it done by a professional. There's nothing like a bad dye job to bring out the best in gay wit—at your expense. Also, stick within your own color range. Brunettes with blond ambitions too often end up looking like citrus fruit. Tragic.

4. If a hairy back is a problem, use a razor, electrolysis, waxing, whichever you like, just do something—unless your better half likes it, which, believe it or not, some do.

5. Use a soft touch with the bronzer, cover-up, and like products. These little helpers may be the poor man's facelift, but a little goes a long way, and too often they end up all over your clothing and everyone around you.

6. Cursed with the dreaded single, monolithic eyebrow? Don't be squeamish about testing out some tweezers (with a stiff drink nearby). But don't go overboard, or you could find yourself resembling Agnes Moorehead.

TO PIERCE OR NOT TO PIERCE

Piercing is no longer the political statement it once was. Pioneered by gay men, it has become *the* thing to do for many of the young *90210* crowd. No longer relegated to the earlobe, studs and hoops are finding themselves in all sorts of interesting places.

At one time, people thought they could tell if a guy was gay by which ear was pierced. Now, with many guys having both ears pierced, often several times over, things aren't so simplistic (not that they ever were). If you decide you have the stomach for piercing (literally or otherwise), pick a body part that jibes with both your professional and personal life. Consulting a doctor is a good idea, particularly if you're thinking about piercing something other than an ear.

Perhaps the leading non-medical authorities on piercing are the folks at The Gauntlet (New York, L.A., San Francisco, and mail order). Having performed over 75,000 piercings, The Gauntlet can probably answer most of your questions. It has even published a free pamphlet, "The Piercing Questions You Keep Asking." You can contact The Gauntlet at (212) 229-0180 (New York), (310) 657-6677 (L.A.), or (415) 592-9715 (mail order). Whether you opt for an ear, two, or something that would make Robert Mapplethorpe proud, the hole can always grow back, can't it?

THE RISKS OF OVEREXPOSURE

Like any other celebutante, one of the biggest mistakes a gay man can make is to become overexposed. The temptation is irresistible to guys who are gluttons for attention. Are you getting so well known that nobody wants to get near you? Do you *always* dance shirtless on the go-go boxes at the bar, your every move carefully choreographed at home in front of a full-length mirror? Is your place in the sun becoming a little too bright?

As one gay man who has been overexposed for years put it, "You know it's time to leave town when you go into a back room for an anonymous encounter and everyone knows your name."

Once a guy has become overexposed, his every action is subjected to the utmost scrutiny by a public just itching to see him fall. Overnight, he goes from hipster to has-been, from a must on everyone's party list to a pariah. If it could happen to Madonna, it can happen to anyone. Don't let it happen to you. Stay home once in a while. Fight the urge to hog the spotlight. Keep a low profile some of the time. In the long run, it pays.

CHAPTER IV
SCALAMANDRÉ AND THE SINGLE GUY
Setting Up House

"You think new curtains are enough to please me!"
—ANN BLYTH, IN *MILDRED PIERCE*

He's young, he's got disposable income, and he's moving to a big city near you—the single gay male. At the top of his to-do list: setting up house.

More than the typical bachelor pad, a gay man's home is a distinctive place that reflects his unique vision of good taste and (most importantly) makes the right impression on the guys he invites over. Creating such a lair requires attention to even the most minute detail, from the right lighting (indirect) and suitable stereo (with tape-to-tape dubbing and remote), to the best bedding (*anything* from Ralph Lauren), tchotchkes (museum replicas), and coffee table books (Impressionists or Mapplethorpe). If such details don't tell your straight neighbor that you're not blind-date material for his maiden sister, maybe the photographs of you cavorting with the boys in tasteful frames on every flat surface in the apartment will.

For those who aren't royalty, but aspire to live like a queen, this chapter will reveal some of the tricks of the trade, as it were, so that you can give the impression you hired a designer without going to the expense of actually doing so. Of course, if your mother sees your new floral chintz slip covers and bursts into tears, you may have gone too far.

CHOOSING THE RIGHT ADDRESS

The most (and maybe only) honest thing a realtor has ever said is, "Location, location, location." In gay terms, this means that *where* you wake up every morning may be a more reliable source of happiness than *who* you wake up with. How many new gays in town have leased an apartment in a complex full of young singles, only to learn (to their immense horror) that they've landed in the midst of hetero Club Dread: weeknight mixers and weekend mixed doubles tournaments; perky secretaries with skimpy running shorts and beer-gutted good ol' boys looking for someone to play foosball with in the clubhouse. It's enough to make your *Anthurium* wilt. Grab your Herb Ritts posters and get the hell outta there.

When scoping out potential neighborhoods, most gays don't put much emphasis on schools; instead, choice gay addresses offer exciting nightlife, good shopping, sophisticated people and, of course, a nearby place to cruise and be cruised. A lot of guys would settle for any place with hot men and a Bloomingdale's (not necessarily in that order).

STATES, CITIES, AND COUNTIES WITH LAWS AGAINST EMPLOYMENT DISCRIMINATION AGAINST GAYS*

We may be royalty, but most of us regrettably have to earn a living. For those too old to have a sugar daddy, it's important to live in a place where at least you know you can't lose your job because of your sexual orientation.

California	Colorado	Maryland
Massachusetts	Michigan	Minnesota
New Mexico	New York	Ohio
Pennsylvania	Rhode Island	Washington
Wisconsin	Alexandria, VA	Alfred, NY
Amherst, MA	Ann Arbor, MI	Aspen, CO
Atlanta, GA	Austin, TX	Baltimore, MD
Berkeley, CA	Boston, MA	Boulder, CO
Buffalo, NY	Burlington, VT	Cambridge, MD
Champaign, IL	Chapel Hill, NC	Chicago, IL
Columbus, OH	Cupertino, CA	Davis, CA
Dayton, OH	Denver, CO	Detroit, MI
East Hampton, NY	East Lansing, MI	Evanston, IL
Gaithersburg, MD	Harrisburg, PA	Hartford, CT
Honolulu, HI	Iowa City, IA	Ithaca, NY
Laguna Beach, CA	Los Angeles, CA	Madison, WI

*__Note:__ Some of these localities only prohibit government employers from discriminating; others prohibit discrimination by private employers as well. With all the ballot referendums out there, check out the laws of your own hometown to be sure.

Malden, MA	Marshall, MN	Milwaukee, WI
Minneapolis, MN	Mountain View, CA	New York, NY
Oakland, CA	Olympia, CA	Palo Alto, CA
Philadelphia, PA	Portland, OR	Pullman, WA
Raleigh, NC	Rochester, NY	Sacramento, CA
Saginaw, MI	San Francisco, CA	Santa Barbara, CA
Santa Cruz, CA	Seattle, WA	Troy, NY
Tucson, AZ	Urbana, IL	Washington, D.C.
West Hollywood, CA	Yellow Springs, OH	Arlington Co., VA
Clallam Co., WA	Cuyahoga Co., OH	Dane Co., WI
Essex Co., NJ	Hennepin Co., MN	Howard Co., MD
Ingham Co., MI	King Co., WA	Minnehaha Co., SD
Montgomery Co., MD	Multnomah Co., OR	Northampton Co., PA
San Mateo Co., CA	Santa Barbara Co., CA	Santa Cruz Co., CA
Suffolk County, NY		

Other places did, but repealed them:

Oregon	Duluth, MN	Eugene, OR
Houston, TX	Lewiston, ME	Lincoln, NE
Miami, FL	St. Paul, MN	San Jose, CA
Wichita, KS		

LIFE AMONG THE NATIVES: THE PROS AND CONS OF THE GAY GHETTO

Even most straights know that 90210 is Beverly Hills. But how many give that knowing glance upon hearing 20009? Those versed in such esoterica recognize it as Dupont Circle (aka the Fruit Loop) and Adams Morgan (Madam's Organ)—Washington, D.C.'s gay ghetto.

Every major city has at least one. In New York, it's Chelsea or the Village; in L.A., it's West Hollywood (once called "Boys Town") or Silver Lake; in Chicago, it's Lakeview; Philadelphia has Spruce Street; San Francisco, the Castro; Boston, the South End; Minneapolis, Loring Hill; Houston, Montrose; Denver, the Capitol District, and so on. For many men, the local gay ghetto is the address of choice. And who wouldn't want to be surrounded by an army of potential playmates and great places to play?

PROS:	CONS:
Scenic views.	You may keep running into that regrettable trick from the night before.
Gay ghettos are often in "transitional" areas with opportunities to buy low and sell high.	"Transitional" may mean going from bad to worse. If you need the Club™ on your car and a vicious rottweiler for a roommate, maybe you should look elsewhere.
Sometimes the gay ghetto is in one of the more *exclusive* neighborhoods.	Exclusivity doesn't count for much if you're house-poor, it's 98 degrees, and all your friends are at the beach.
It has the best bars and trendiest restaurants in town . . .	. . . if you can afford them.
Security—there's strength in numbers. You have the freedom to greet friends on the street with a kiss.	Walking hand-in-hand down Christoper Street is great, but it may not go over as well on Main Street.
Gay-owned or gay-friendly card shops and clothing stores with distinctly gay merchandise.	Do you think you can wear those skintight Lycra hotpants anywhere but the gay ghetto?
A real feeling of community.	You may get more than enough community at the gym.
Total immersion in *the scene.*	Total immersion in *the scene.*

SEARCHING FOR SIGNS OF INTELLIGENT LIFE: LIVING IN SUBURBIA AND BEYOND

"You could move."
—ABIGAIL VAN BUREN ("DEAR ABBY"),
RESPONDING TO A READER WHO, AFTER RANTING
ABOUT A GAY COUPLE'S MOVING IN ACROSS THE
STREET, ASKED, "HOW CAN WE IMPROVE THE
QUALITY OF THE . . . NEIGHBORHOOD?"

Despite the concentrated camaraderie of the gay ghetto, many men shun the bright lights of the big city and opt for the less hectic environs of the suburbs. What with the chorus of lawnmowers on Saturday mornings, the security of opening ground-floor windows without burglar bars, and the tanning potential of a real backyard, little wonder so many gay men gravitate toward suburbia and small-town America.

But gay men who choose to live among Laura & Rob and Edith & Archie may give up some of the anonymity of urban life and expose themselves to the curiosity of their excitement-starved neighbors. Living next door to Dan and Roseanne, gay suburbanites may do as much or more to change straight America's misconceptions about gays as their more vocal urban brothers do. Soon enough, those neighbors who hummed "Where the Boys Are" each time they passed by will realize that a gay neighbor has something to offer everyone—expert gardening advice for the men and creative things to do with zucchini for the ladies.

No matter how comfortable a guy becomes with being a neighborhood celebrity, strip malls and casserole dishes are no substitute for socializing with other gay men. Straight people just aren't that much fun. Luckily, regardless of where they live, gay men have a knack for finding other guys who enjoy making fresh pasta. Contrary to the jaded misperceptions of some city dwellers, you don't have to come into the city to have a gay social life. If you're a newly minted suburbanite, just try the local gourmet shop, farmers' market, garden center, or—if all else fails—the "Y."

THE COUNTRY GIRL:
A SURVIVAL KIT FOR RURAL LIVING

Some of the more privileged of our set spend their weekends at their country retreats, living out their fantasy of the hunt, ambling about in jodhpurs and tweed in "cottages" crammed with English hunt scenes and Ralph Lauren *nouveau* "heirlooms." For these queens, "roughing it" means a grocery store that doesn't deliver. They think any gay man who *lives* in the country must be like Eva Gabor in "Green Acres." Not so.

True country boys opt for rural life *full time*. They prefer the rustic lifestyle and slower pace. And they *like* being one of five gay men in their county. The fresh smell of country days and the starry stillness of country nights are more appealing to them than any smoke-filled, video-assaulted happy hour spot in the city's gay ghetto.

But for those who've *recently* moved to the country, and aren't quite ready to trade symphony concerts for tractor pulls, here are a few things to ensure your survival, if not your sanity:

1. A four-wheel-drive vehicle. Ask the lesbians down the road which model to buy.

2. A WATS line. How else can you keep track of who your friends in the city are sleeping with?

3. Directions to the nearest gay bar—plus food and water (and maybe a compass) for the journey.

4. Subscriptions to regional and national gay magazines and newspapers. How else would you know that those platform shoes in the back of your closet are in style again? (They'll really love them at the farmers' co-op.)

5. A sizable pornography collection; nights in the country can get a little lonely.

6. A tape of All About Eve *to keep your claws sharpened.*

7. A directory of 976 chat lines. You can't rely on the annual ice cream social in town for your sole source of human (especially gay) contact.

GAY CITIES

Gay, GA	Gay, KY	Gay, MI
Gays, IL	Gayville, SD	Gaysville, VT
Gays Creek, KY	Gays Mills, WI	Fort Gay, WY
Fruitland, MD	Fruitvale, ID	Dyke, VA
Dike, TX	Ferrysburg, MI	Queens, NY

A QUEEN'S HOME IS HIS CASTLE: MUST HAVES FOR THE PERFECT PAD

"What a dump!"
—BETTE DAVIS, IN *BEYOND THE FOREST*

Many gay men's homes, for all their uniqueness and creativity, share a lot of similarities. Whether you're in San Francisco, Minneapolis, or Atlanta, look carefully, and you'll likely see many of the same elements: ☞

The Living Room:

1. gilt mirror (there can never be enough mirrors in the home); **silk <u>ficus</u>** (<u>very</u> low maintenance); **marble obelisks** (subconscious attraction to them); **crystal clock** (gift from an older admirer);

2. kentia palm (subtle jungle imagery), **<u>Spathiphyllum,</u>** and other dramatic **low-light plants** in **terra-cotta pots** with garland and <u>putti</u> or in big **wicker baskets** from Pier One (plants are the best companions; they don't eat much, never have to be walked, and never talk back); real or <u>faux</u> **fireplace** (creates atmosphere; good seduction potential), with unburned decorative **white birch logs** on grill;

3. stereo with CD player, tape-to-tape dubbing (for bootlegging DJ tapes), and **hidden speakers** (they're ugly); **apothecary lamp** (creates flattering indirect lighting); overstuffed **sofa with Brunschwig & Fils fabric** (conveniently pulls out to queen-size bed); politically correct **<u>faux</u> leopard print pillows** (showing bold masculinity, tempered by **Scalamandré silk fringe**); **original art** by a friend, with **portrait light,** lending appearance of greater value;

4. glass- or **marble-top coffee table** with **replica column capital base** (glass helps reflect indirect lighting); **coffee table books** (Impressionist painters and Mapplethorpe photographs create image of refinement, balanced by Bruce Weber or Ken Haak beefcake); **dhurrie** or **Oriental rug; <u>potpourri</u>** (the only thing worse than bad breath is "houseatosis"); slightly burned **candles** in **silver or crystal candlesticks** (it's considered impolite to have new, unburned candles when you have company); **fresh flowers** in **crystal vase** with **glass marbles** in bottom (mandatory); **crystal bowl** (another gift from the same older admirer—he wants something);

5. skirted table (skirt hides fact that it's not really a table) with non-specific **objets d'art** and **museum replicas;** framed **photos of self,** self with friends, self with family;

6. track lighting on rheostats; botanical prints (not expensive but look it);

7. slipper chair (for holding court) with **needlepoint pillow;** pile of **approved magazines** (see below).

The Kitchen:

1. <u>**Men of USC**</u> **calendar; phone with extra-long cord** (much time spent on the phone while cooking); **cork board** with **party invitations** (for guests to see);

2. freezer/refrigerator with **photos of self,** self with friends, self with family, in magnetized frames; contents of freezer: **Absolut Vodka, boneless chicken breasts, Lean Cuisines, coffee,** and **fresh pasta;** contents of refrigerator: **champagne, bottled water, cranberry juice, 1/2 lime; skim milk** for coffee; **glass-front cabinets,** lit from within, showcasing **china; Le Creuset** and **Calphalon** pots and pans (gay status symbols);

3. granite or granite-like Corian worktop with **champagne flutes, highball, double old-fashioned,** and **on-the-rocks glasses** (commitment in crystal to entertaining; friends like to drink);

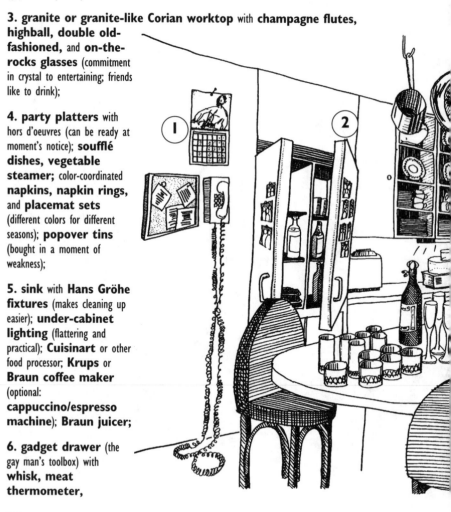

4. party platters with hors d'oeuvres (can be ready at moment's notice); **soufflé dishes, vegetable steamer;** color-coordinated **napkins, napkin rings,** and **placemat sets** (different colors for different seasons); **popover tins** (bought in a moment of weakness);

5. sink with **Hans Gröhe fixtures** (makes cleaning up easier); **under-cabinet lighting** (flattering and practical); **Cuisinart** or other food processor; **Krups** or **Braun coffee maker** (optional: **cappuccino/espresso machine); Braun juicer;**

6. gadget drawer (the gay man's toolbox) with **whisk, meat thermometer,**

skewers, **tea strainer, cheese knives, chopsticks, garlic press, pastry blender, pastry brush, melon baller, grapefruit knife, shrimp peeler, champagne re-corker, citrus zester,** and other items used once;

7. rack with **wineglasses, cordial glasses** (for <u>important</u> dinner parties); **built-in wine rack** for easy access;

8. cooktop with built-in **grill; under-cabinet microwave** (leaves countertops clear for decorative tchotchkes);

9. cookbooks: <u>Silver Palate</u>, Julia Child's **<u>The Way to Cook</u>, <u>The Joy of Cooking</u>, <u>La Varenne Pratique</u>** (most never opened); back issues of **<u>Gourmet</u>** and **<u>Bon Appétit</u>** (most never read).

The Bedroom:

1. dramatic **dark walls** with **light-colored molding**; non-utilitarian **designer window treatments** draped just so; real **<u>Ficus benjaminus</u>** (good light in bedroom);

2. real or <u>faux</u> **antique bachelor's chest** with **clean T-shirts, socks,** and **small towels, lubricant, condoms,** and **sexy magazines**; partially burned **Rigaud** and other **candles** for mood setting; **antique-like lamp sconces; wooden-framed mirror** (movable);

3. designer or **designer-look luggage** under bed (used as much as accent pieces as for travel); **"Oriental"** rug of dubious origin; **gym bag**;

4. queen-size sleigh bed with **designer bedding** (**Ralph Lauren** or **Pratesi**); **down pillows, comforter,** or **duvet; American** and **European** (square) **pillows** with **contrasting pillow shams;** monogrammed **throw pillows;**

5. traditional-look armoire (circa 1992), built as an entertainment center with **TV, VCR, blue videos; photographs of self** and **mother's wedding picture** in a variety of **tasteful frames** (unimaginative friends give frames every holiday);

6. huge closet with **closet organizers;** more **shoes** than Imelda Marcos; more **ties** than Countess Mara; **sweaters** in every shade; **plush robe; shirts** and **jackets** arranged by color and style; slimming **full-length mirror** behind closet door;

7. reading chair with **ottoman** and **throw pillow** with Alice Longworth quote: "If you don't have anything nice to say about anyone, come sit by me."; **cordless phone** (huge range for maximum conversational convenience) and **answering machine** (hard to decorate around, but essential where Voice Mail is unavailable); **architectural prints** (masculine, cultured-looking);

8. traditional **low chest** with carefully displayed **Playbill** from most recent popular theatrical debut; **wallet** and **checkbook** (both **Coach**); **Swatches,** knock-off **Rolex,** and bandannas.

"[T]he bathroom is the giveaway, the fantasy-killer . . . Face creams and shampoos for *days*. And on the top of the toilet tank they've all always got one of those goddamn little gold pedestals full of colored soap balls!"

—MICHAEL TOLLIVER, IN ARMISTEAD MAUPIN'S *TALES OF THE CITY*

MAKING A HOUSE A HOME:
IT'S THE LITTLE THINGS THAT COUNT

"My taste is impeccable, even when it's bad!"
—**ALAN BATES, IN** *NIJINSKY*

Competition for the *most* perfect gay home is intense. When gay friends visit, the white gloves come off and your place receives an unspoken inspection that rivals a Marine sergeant's on parade day. But all the Scalamandré silk tassels and Clarence House fabrics in the world are nothing without the right cultural components. Appropriate literature, periodicals, and music are essential to make a gay man's house his home. Your friends will duly note the books on your shelves, magazines in your powder room, and music you play, and discuss them in detail after they leave. If you don't want your friends to think you're a philistine, but don't know where to begin, some suggestions:

TWELVE BOOKS EVERY GAY MAN SHOULD READ (OR AT LEAST HAVE ON HIS COFFEE TABLE)

1. **Becoming a Man**, by Paul Monette—A funny yet powerful autobiography and coming-to-grips-with-it story. The only gay story by a gay author to win the National Book Award. Almost impossible to put down.

2. **Dancer from the Dance**, by Andrew Holleran—Malone emerges from his solitary existence as a corporate lawyer, enters the New York club scene of the '70s with a vengeance, and goes through a string of relationships only to end up selling his services (*not* his *legal* services). A bit dated now after the cold shower of the '80s, but it's been called *The Great Gatsby* of gay life.

3. **Eighty-Sixed**, by David B. Feinberg—A hilariously realistic, but justifiably cynical, look at gay life in New York in two distinctly different years—1980 and '86. The title is a reference to what AIDS did to gay life as we knew it.

4. **Leaves of Grass**, by Walt Whitman—Called "the most revolutionary figure in modern poetry," brother Walt *Leaves* you breathless, especially with "I Sing the Body Electric," an ode to man's body.

5. **Looking Good** and/or **Working Out**, by Charles Hix (photos by Ken Haak)—For years, the stuff of which many gay men's fantasies were made. Practical, useful advice on grooming, wardrobe, and fitness, with pictures to die for.

6. **Maurice**, by E. M. Forster—The author of *A Passage to India* and *A Room with a View* took a big risk with this 1913 novel about gay love that actually has a happy romantic ending. (Happiness was off-limits to gays in those days.) Given the times, the book wasn't published until after Forster died. Read the book, then see the movie.

7. **Remembrance of Things Past**, by Marcel Proust—So what if it's three volumes and three thousand pages? It's actually a series of seven novels in which virtually all the leading male characters turn out to be gay. What with the gym and your active social life, you may not have time to read it all, but it will look *so* impressive on the shelf. Especially in the original French, *n'est-ce pas?*

8. **28 Barbary Lane (Tales of the City Omnibus)**, by Armistead Maupin—Mary Ann moves to San Francisco and finds herself embroiled in the lives and loves of an apartment house full of eccentric characters. Will Michael find true love with another man? Will Mary Ann be disgusted and move back to Cleveland? Is Mrs. Madrigal a man in drag? Read it and see. Better than "Melrose Place"; Maupin's *proud* of his gay characters.

9. **The Amy Vanderbilt Complete Book of Etiquette,** entirely rewritten and updated by Nancy Tuckerman and Nancy Dunnan—If you take pride in your china, silver, and crystal, you'd better know which fork to use as well as how to deal with many other sticky social situations. This book can provide some assistance. If only straight people would use it.

10. **The Front Runner,** by Patricia Nell Warren—Strapping young Billy thinks his greatest love is track until he meets Coach. The jockstraps come off fast, and it's not long

The Makings of a Gay Nightmare

The Night the China Cabinet Crashed!

before the world knows that Olympian-in-the-making Billy and his Coach are slipping each other more than just the relay baton. Oh, *l'amour, l'amour!*

11. **The Gay Book of Days**, by Martin Greif—Well-documented mini-biographies of famous (and infamous) gay men and lesbians in history. A must-read for those whose gay pride needs a boost.

12. **The Movie Lover**, by Richard Friedel—Burton Raider would rather watch old Jean Harlow movies than play touch football with the neighborhood boys. Hunky Roman DeMarco moves in next door and the fun begins in this hilarious story of a young man's coming out and of age. Raider gets the tiara as one of the wittiest gay characters in fiction.

ELEVEN MAGAZINES EVERY GAY MAN SHOULD GET

1. **The Advocate**—Still the most authoritative and respected national gay and lesbian news magazine.

2. **Out, Genre, 10 Percent**—Relatively recent arrivals to the newsstand, all three seem to aim toward a more mainstream format than the traditional gay press. Support one or all of them and the companies advertising in their pages. They know what side their croissant is buttered on.

3. **Vanity Fair**—The thinking man's gossip rag; what with the Annie Leibovitz visuals and the best, or at least most unusual, horoscopes, it's the source of many cocktail party conversations. A-Listers generally prefer *Town & Country*'s high-society news and zodiac advice; besides, they may have dated some of the grooms featured in its wedding announcements.

4. **Men's Fitness**—Whether or not you work out, it's a must. Its pages are filled with incredible physiques in tantalizing poses and gym wear. Even a truly straight guy would sneak a second look. If you're a bit more "mature" and actually want to read about the latest in hair loss research, go for *Men's Health*.

5. **Details**—Targeted to the younger reader, it merits mention as perhaps the only "mainstream" magazine that doesn't ignore its gay readers. (See *GQ*, below.) Older readers may find the fashions bordering on the absurd, but it covers the latest in pop culture, including progressive tunes and clubs for disco bunnies of all ages.

6. **Architectural Digest**—Or **Metropolitan Home**, if your aspirations are more realistic. Gay men have driven store clerks crazy trying to mix paint for their dining room walls that matches the "Squash Blossom" bedroom in last month's edition. You may actually know some of the designers featured.

7. **Entertainment Weekly**—The real news. "Entertainment Tonight" that you can read on the subway. If you just *have*

to know what happened during the filming of *Philadelphia,* or why Anne Rice gnashed her teeth over the choice of Tom Cruise as the Vampire LeStat, this is the place for the poop. Also covers TV, music, videos, and books. It's addictive, but expensive.

8. **GQ**—Unable to decide if it's *The Atlantic* or *Cosmopolitan* for men. True, many wouldn't be caught dead in the clothes featured in its pages (or couldn't afford them if they wanted to), but the editors' attempt to make topics such as "The Male G-spot" and "What to do with Problem Cuticles" interesting to the "straight" reader are worth the look.

9. **Gourmet**—With entertaining such a critical part of gay life, "The Magazine of Good Living," as it is otherwise known, can be a source for menu ideas that will keep them talking for weeks. A bit heavy-handed on the expensive travel news, however. For those with limited means who find themselves spending more time in the kitchen than on the beach in Bali, check out *Bon Appétit* or *Food & Wine.*

10. **Travel & Leisure**—Two of the three favorite pursuits of gay men. After you've spent all that time pumping and primping, you don't want to waste it on the same tired old happy hour crowd. You owe it to yourself *and* the world to make public appearances all over the globe. This and others such as *Condé Nast Traveler* will help you do it in style.

11. **People**—There are a lot of closet *People* readers out there. You hate to admit it, but how else can you keep up with Liz and Larry, Diana and Charles, and Loni and Burt? Its annual "Sexiest Man Alive" edition is a collector's item. Those who really want to get under (or a glimpse of) the skin of the latest star or starlet often opt for *Interview* instead.

SIXTEEN CDS EVERY GAY MAN SHOULD OWN

"I think that a lifetime of listening to disco music is a high price to pay for one's sexual preference."

—QUENTIN CRISP

1. **Bronski Beat, <u>Age of Consent</u>**—Revolutionary activist rock and dance music from the first out-in-your-face group to make it big. The album liner was a primer on worldwide age-of-consent laws. If only it wasn't so hard to stuff in your back pocket.

2. **Patsy Cline, <u>12 Greatest Hits</u>**—Before the dance divas of the '70s and '80s, there was Patsy, and gay men have been "Crazy" for her ever since. A great sampler of her most memorable work.

3. **Erasure, <u>The Innocents</u>**—Gay men singing about gay love. If you're really a fan, rent one of their concert videos; the lead singer, Andy Bell, could make anyone feel butch.

4. **Ella Fitzgerald, <u>The Rodgers and Hart Song Book, Vols. I & II</u>**—Of the eight Ella "songbooks," this may be *the* gay favorite, with memorable renditions of "You Took Advantage of Me" and "The Lady Is a Tramp."

5. **Judy Garland, <u>Judy at Carnegie Hall</u>**—"Quiet please, there's a lady on stage." Perhaps the best-selling concert album of all time. Buy it, and you'll understand why her death is said to have sparked Stonewall. If you don't like live albums, check out *Little Girl Blue.*

6. **Deborah Harry & Blondie, <u>The Complete Picture</u>**—Songs like "Call Me" and "I Want That Man" make this a gay must-have. Listening to it will make many re-live their youths. Can you stand it?

7. **Madonna, <u>The Immaculate Collection</u>**—Gay men will always have a special place in their hearts for Madonna, once the goddess of dance music. (Her "Respect Yourself" and "Cherish" videos are soft porn classics.) Own this and you'll have all the Material Girl you'll ever need. Or be able to stomach.

8. **Neville Mariner, conducting Academy of St. Martin in the Fields, <u>Water Music</u>**—Written for an all-night royal boat party nearly three hundred years ago, Handel's regal Water Music continues to soothe modern-day queens after all-night dancing on a speaker or an evening with their lover's mother.

9. **Bette Midler, <u>The Divine Miss M</u>**—Though the younger set may only know her from *Beaches* and *Down and Out in Beverly Hills,* the rest of us know that singing in the baths really made her famous. This is her best work. Ever.

10. **Liza Minnelli, <u>Liza with a "Z"</u>**—Mz. Minnelli's live TV coming out performance—before she married songstress Peter Allen, and while she was dating then-hunk Desi Arnaz, Jr. Gay men swooned.

11. **Original Broadway Cast, <u>Gypsy</u>**—Whether you're a theater queen or not, you've gotta have at least one of Broadway's classics for those nights around the piano bar. Might as well get the best. With Ethel Merman in the lead, legions of drag queens followed.

12. **Moodswings, <u>Moodfood</u>**—Perfect for morning parties, those after-the-bar get-togethers that have recently become *the* thing in some circles. If you're worn out from dancing, but not quite ready to come back to earth, its dramatic sounds and primal rhythms will give you something to focus on.

13. **The Pet Shop Boys, <u>Discography: The Complete Singles Collection</u>**—Songs like these brought an entire generation back to the dance floor after the decline of disco, and led to the evolution of the post-modern Club Kid.

14. **Renata Scotto, et al., <u>Madama Butterfly</u>**—Sooner or later all gay men experience an undeniable urge to hear opera. (It *must* be genetic.) If you're not already into it, start off right with Puccini's melodious story of East meeting West. Every gay man has surely heard this line before, but: Try it, you'll like it.

15. **Barbra Streisand, <u>Just for the Record . . .</u>**—All right, all right, four CDs is an awful lot of Barbra, but program the tracks you like best, and it'll be like buttah.

16. **Sylvester, <u>Greatest Hits: Non-Stop Dance Party</u>**—He may be gone, but he's not forgotten. Luckily he left us with camp dance classics that will make generations of gay men gyrate.

WHY PAY RETAIL?
(CULTIVATING DESIGNER FRIENDS)

Decorating your home is an expensive proposition, but it doesn't have to be if you're gay. Hard as it may be to believe, many interior designers *are* gay. You probably know some or have even dated one or two. Capitalize on it. Do

you know what the markup is on that stuff? How else do you think they pay for their Jaguars and beach houses?

Befriending an interior designer could save you big bucks when furnishing your home. Designer friends can offer helpful—and free—advice on the right color rug to complement the *moiré* couch you just ordered. Or, if you tried to paint your living room *caffe latte* but it turned out looking like orange sherbet, who better to invite over for some emergency interior design advice than a professional? Designers *do* make house calls, especially if there's a cocktail waiting for them. If you play your cards right, you may be able to get a few items at cost. Sleep with him and you may never see a bill.

Where to Shop

The single most valuable resource for decorating your home is the Design Center, a one-stop showroom paradise for real and would-be designers. There's a Design Center in most major cities—New York, L.A., Houston, Chicago, Dallas, Miami, San Francisco, and Washington, to name a few—but it sometimes goes by a different name. In New York, it's the D & D (Decoration and Design Building); in Chicago, the Merchandise Mart; and L.A.'s Pacific Design Center is affectionately known as the "Blue Whale."

The only problem with the Design Centers (besides the prices) is that many of them won't allow the public in without a designer. (At least that's what they *seem* to mean by "to the trade only," although there *are* always legions of handsome young men hanging around those places with no apparent purpose.) Yet another reason to cultivate designer friends. Acceptable (and often less expensive) alternatives to the Design Centers are antique shows, flea markets, auctions, and estate sales. Watch the local papers. Two of the biggest flea markets are held in Atlanta (all weekend) and New York (Sundays only). New York's can be found around 26th and 6th; Atlanta's is on Peachtree Industrial Boulevard.

If you *must* shop at a chain, be prepared to see your prized possessions *everywhere*. Approved chains include the Pottery Barn, Williams-Sonoma, and Domaine. Of course, for a more generic (though acceptable) look, there's always Crate & Barrel and Ikea. You could spend an entire day in Chicago's Michigan Avenue Crate & Barrel.

Those in serious contention for a spot in the pages of *Metropolitan Home* will need to use a bit more imagination in their decorating. For them, some suggestions:

ABC Carpet, Furniture and Home—Broadway at 19th, New York. If you can't find it here, you can't find it anywhere.

Art FX—King Street, Alexandria, VA (outside Washington). Eye-catching neoclassical pieces not likely to be seen in many straight homes. The management likes our kind.

Civilization—Venice Blvd., Culver City (L.A.). 25,000 square feet of unique or almost unique collector's items, many made by local artists.

Cobweb—West Houston, New York. Mostly cool antique imports, primarily furniture.

Distinctive Furnishings—Bleecker Street, New York. Small and cozy, like a Merchant & Ivory film, rich handmade pillows and other accent pieces at irresistible prices.

Gump's—Union Square, San Francisco. If you're vying with your sister for Mom's china, and Sis has the upper hand, no bother. You'll find over four hundred china patterns here. A mandatory stop for those on their way to a wedding.

Harry Furniture—Venice Blvd., Culver City (L.A.). The '40s, '50s, and '60s thrive in this museum to questionable taste. If you're the adventurous decorator type or just want to gawk, it's worth a visit.

Heyday—E. 7th Street, New York. For those who want to live like they're in the country but can't give up the city, the country primitive collectables here will bridge the gap.

Homebodies—N. Halstead Street, Chicago. Couches, candles, cards, and everything in between. Very hip, in the heart of Chicago's gay ghetto.

Innovations—Monroe Drive, Atlanta. Modern classic furniture for gracious but cool Southern living.

Janice Aldrich—M Street, Washington. Classic oils, prints, and architectural renderings. The real thing, with surreal prices.

Little Rickie—First Avenue at Third, New York. Glow-in-the-dark Elvis lamps, Haitian picture frames, and other unusual items for those who don't take their decorating too seriously.

Portico Home Furnishings, Bed & Bath—West Broadway, New York. Great sheets and a coffee bar to boot.

Room and Board—Michigan Avenue, Chicago. Dramatic, largely contemporary, furniture and accessories. Ikea with flair and hungrier cash registers.

Skynear & Co.—Wyoming Avenue and 18th Street, Washington. One of the most eclectic collections of furniture and accent pieces, handsomely displayed in a large bright town house minutes from the White House.

Z Gallerie—Union Street, San Francisco; Melrose Avenue, L.A. Contemporary furnishings and conversation pieces for the in-crowd. Very "Melrose Place."

DECK THE HALLS—
DECORATING FOR THE HOLIDAYS

While straight men are fixated on the final stretch of the NFL season, gay men are engrossed in their own competitive sport—decorating their homes for the holidays. A time-consuming and expensive undertaking, decking the halls of a gay man's home typically means more white lights, garland, and bows than Martha Stewart and her glue gun could begin to handle. Christmas trees are thematic, often overwhelmed with crystal, beads, or lace. And candles, by the dozen, provide just the right amount of reflected light (off the crystal on the tree). Done well, a gay man's home becomes a veritable winter wonderland at the holidays. But if a guy's desire to

"haul out the holly" gets out of hand, his home could end up looking like Santa threw up all over it.

With his halls decked, the gay man sets out on a grueling gauntlet of Christmas open houses where he and his friends keep mental score and feign oo-ing and ahing at each other's artistic interpretations: the Little Drummer Boy made of dried fruits and grasses, the Three Wise Men cloaked in handmade bugle-beaded robes, a model of Bethlehem as the Emerald City. The holidays bring out the frustrated window dresser in all of us. Just don't give up the day job.

STRAIGHTENING UP: DE-GAYING THE HOME FOR STRAIGHT VISITORS (A CHECKLIST)

"Housework is like bad sex. Every time I do it, I swear I'll never do it again, until company comes by."
—PARTY GUEST, IN *CAN'T STOP THE MUSIC*

All gay men love to entertain, and occasionally that means having family members or friends over who haven't quite dealt with the fact that their host is "you know, *that* way." As fun as it may be to imagine letting your prudish Aunt Thelma see the "Jeff with Tires" and Soloflex posters on your walls and the Wet Jockey Shorts Party invitation taped to your refrigerator door, if you're not well versed in CPR or don't have a good attorney, better to anticipate potential shockers before they happen, especially if you're not sure you're in the will yet. The longer you've been out, the harder it will be to identify items with the capacity to stop pacemakers. For this reason, a checklist:

1. Put away your pornography. (Don't forget the tape that's been in the VCR since last weekend; your guest could think that *Giants* is an Elizabeth Taylor film and be in for a *big* surprise.)

2. Turn down the volume on your answering machine or disconnect it. Think about some of the messages your friends leave for you and imagine your guest hearing them. Granted, it would make a funny movie scene, but not in *your* life.

3. Temporarily replace the pictures of you and your latest lover frolicking in the surf. And while you're at it, ditch a few of those photos of you in doe-eyed, model-like poses. You don't want your guest thinking you're really *that* narcissistic.

4. Clear your coffee table of any soft-porn pictorials—*Bear Pond, Sleeping Beauties, Extraordinary Friends*—and take down the "Men of USC" calendar hanging in your kitchen. Saying you "appreciate good photography" won't cut it when all the pictures are of half-naked men.

5. If possible, lock your bathroom cabinet. Unsensitized straight people would be hard-pressed to understand the need for bronzer; and all the mousses, gels, spritzes, and sculpting lotions might make them a tad suspicious.

6. Make sure that Diana Ross number you wore last Halloween is put away. Way away. Drag at Halloween may come naturally to gay men, but straights tend to stick to conventional costumes, like teenage ninja turtles, or scary ones, like Ronald Reagan.

GAY ISN'T	GAY IS
Mickey Mouse	Mykonos
chintzy	chintz
Monday Night Football	*Entertainment Tonight*
drag racing	drag
guilt	gilt
training wheels	personal trainers
Kmart	K-hole
Pop Tarts	poppers
trick-or-treat	tricks
wide receivers	tight ends
KP	K-Y

CHAPTER V

SOMEDAY MY PRINCE WILL COME
Dating in a World of Potential Future Ex-Lovers

The Dating Game of the Gay Nineties isn't as simple as choosing between Bachelor Number 1, 2, or 3. When setting out to find true love, gay men face questions of almost existential proportions—or at least they seem so at the time. Are there sure-fire ways to meet Mr. Right (or at least Mr. Good-for-a-Saturday Night)? Is it possible to find connubial bliss in a gay bar? Why do so many men of steel have heels of helium? Gay men have pondered these questions for years, discussed them *ad nauseam* with their friends, and sent many therapists' kids to private school searching for the answers. Search no more.

The world is full of potential future ex-lovers, but that doesn't make dating any easier. The honeymoon between sex and the single gay male is over; it seems that everyone's in a relationship, and those that aren't are either celibates or sluts. And, when you finally find that millionaire/model/genius of your dreams, he may turn out to be a semi-literate, unemployed psycho-killer. Nevertheless, our very nature drives us to seek out other men—in some cases, lots of them. So swallow your pride, stuff a condom or two in your wallet, and do *something* about that hair. Love is in the air.

TOP TEN TURN-OFFS FOR GUYS LOOKING FOR LOVE

Love is a two-way street. Before you head out in search of your own Prince Charming, make sure you're driving men wild, not away. An informal survey of gay men across the country shows what really turns guys off. The top ten answers are on the board, and the survey says . . .

1. **FEMMES**—Hands down, the number one answer. As one respondent put it, "If I wanted a woman, I'd be straight."

2. **ATTITUDE**—Another big turn-off. Seems most men prefer guys with their feet on the ground to those with their noses in the air (i.e., A-listers need not apply).

3. **SELF-ABSORPTION**—It may be difficult, but try to show some, if only a passing, interest in others.

4. **BAD BODIES**—A gym membership really could pay

off, but only if you spend at least as much time on the weights as you do in the showers.

5. **UNSIGHTLY BODY HAIR**—Respondents varied in their personal pet peeves, but back, ear, and nose hair seem to be the most problematic.

6. **SMOKING**—Kissing an ashtray is not something most gay men find stimulating.

7. **COLOGNE**—Apparently the excessive use of cologne is more widespread than originally thought. One respondent suggested that Karl Lagerfeld be taken out and shot.

8. **NO SENSE OF HUMOR**—A cardinal sin in the gay world.

9. **POOR TASTE IN CLOTHES**—Who said gay men are superficial?

10. **DRINKING WITH A STRAW**—Submitted by one respondent. It's a tough crowd out there.

"Well, let me see... 2 cups of milk, 4 eggs, 1 cup grated Swiss..."

HOW TO TELL A TOP FROM A BOTTOM

Although gay men are generally able to adapt to any situation, when it comes to sex, many still consider themselves *strictly* tops or bottoms. For those rigid fundamentalists, going home with someone of the same preference can mean playing a frustrating game of solitaire rather than five-card stud. Being able to determine, *in advance,* whether a prospective date is a top or bottom is therefore an indispensable skill for those with limited time and imagination. Recognizing that there are exceptions to every rule, some pointers:

1. A **bottom** wears pants that showcase his derrière; a **top** always notices.

2. If a guy drives a truck, he's a **top;** if he drives a cute car, such as a Nissan 240SX, Mazda RX7 or Mazda Miata, he's a **bottom.**

3. The more a guy is obsessed with finding a butch boyfriend, the more likely he's a **bottom.**

4. A **top** eats steak for dinner; a **bottom** has salad.

5. Look at his boots. The heavier the boots, the more likely he is to be a **bottom**. Bottoms need heavy boots to keep their feet on the floor.

6. **Tops** have calloused knees; **bottoms** have calloused elbows.

7. If a guy catches you cruising him, and turns his back, he's showing you his best ass-et—a **bottom;** a guy leaning back against a wall or the bar with his thumbs hooked in his belt loops is fly fishing—a **top.**

8. A **top** has short fingernails, but a **bottom**'s look better.

9. If you ask a guy what he likes to do in the bedroom and he vacillates, or says that he's "versatile," he's a **bottom. Tops** seem to think it's some kind of honor and will always tell you.

10. When in doubt, remember, for every **top** there are ten **bottoms,** or so it seems.

"WHAT'S YOUR SIGN?"
(RESPONDING TO THE MOST OVERUSED PICKUP LINES)

Bad pickup lines are like birthdays. They just keep coming, and we've had so many, we've stopped counting. Spend an evening eavesdropping in a bar and you'll be amazed at how shamelessly these lines are still employed. Less common are responses that tell would-be lotharios you've heard it all before. Some suggestions:

Line: "Haven't we met before?"
Response: "Yes, we have. It was September 8, 1991, and you tried the same line on me then."

Line: "Do you come here often?"
Response: "Not anymore."

Line: "Going home so early?"
Response: "This crowd's tired."

Line: "You should model."
Response: "I do."

Line: "I think you dropped this dollar." (Picking up a dollar bill *he* dropped and offering it to you.)
Response: "Thanks." (Take it.) "See you later."

Line: "Do you live around here?"
Response: "Yes, with two cats, a dog, and my lover."

Line: "That shirt would look good hanging in my closet."
Response: "They don't make it in ladies' sizes."

Line: "Smile. It's not that bad."
Response: "It is now."

Line: "Aren't you on television?"
Response: "Yeah, 'America's Most Wanted.' "

Line: "Do you need a spot?" (at the gym)
Response: "No, thanks, I already have a dog."

Line: "If destiny has its way, you and I will be lovers."
Response: "Not if Destiny's any friend of mine."

READING BETWEEN THE LINES: THE PERSONAL ADS

The personal ads are a tried, though perhaps not true, means of looking for Mr. Goodbar. Browsing through them, the world seems full of promise—everyone is young, built, handsome, and looking for love. Yet, reality often turns out to be a case of Beauty and the Beast: You read about beauty, but a Beast is knocking on your door. Reading the personal ads is like reading stock quotes, box scores, or Shakespeare. To avoid date disaster, a guy has to understand what he's reading. For the inexperienced, some guidelines:

When they say:

Professional GM, versatile teddy bear. My friends tell me I'm handsome. 30ish, straight acting, relationship-oriented, and politically aware, with a strong grasp of humanity. Enjoy working out, children, singing, hiking, mountains, European travel. ISO discreet, young GM, masculine and marine-like; a novice but adventuresome. No fats, femmes, or druggies.

They mean:

Professional: Has a job

GM: Gay male

versatile: Is a bottom

teddy bear: Overweight with more hair than an ape

My friends tell me I'm handsome: You should see his friends

30ish: Early forties

straight acting: Don't call him at work.

relationship-oriented: Clinging vine; black hole of emotional need

politically aware: Registered to vote

strong grasp of humanity: Meaningless, but will impress some

Enjoy working out: Takes an occasional aerobics class, lurks in shower afterward

Enjoy . . . children, singing, hiking, mountains, European travel: Has seen *The Sound of Music* too many times

ISO: In search of

discreet: Won't call him at work

young GM: Chicken; just this side of jail bait

masculine: Is a top

marine-like: Will discipline him

novice: There are still a few things he hasn't tried

adventuresome: Willing to try acrobatic sex

No fats, femmes, or druggies: Last boyfriend was an obese drag queen with a substance abuse problem

GAY RULES OF THUMB

For all the intricacies and complexities of the Gay Dating Game, there are still some universal truths on which you can rely:

1. High hair, low morals. (If you're a Southern queen, the higher the hair, the closer to God.)

2. The later it gets, the better they look.

3. Just because you think you're going home with a handsome guy doesn't mean you're going to wake up with one.

4. Self-absorbed in conversation, self-absorbed in bed.

5. The more financial security a guy claims to have, the less emotional security he has.

6. Man of steel, heels of helium.

7. If he has plenty of gossip *for* you, he has plenty of gossip *about* you.

8. The more they deny, the more they will try.

9. The higher you are, the lower you'll go.

10. The looser they are, the looser they are.

THE AGONY AND THE ECSTASY: RATING FIRST DATES

You finally meet someone who sparks your interest. The next step is the first date. Often, it comes right on the heels of your meeting, within a matter of minutes (if you can call *that* a date). Other times, a period of tortured longing could pass before someone makes a move. Either way, the first date could be the defining moment in a gay relationship. Select it carefully.

The Dinner Out—Pretty standard fare. Make sure you go armed with something to talk about. If he spends more time checking out the waiter than looking at you, don't order dessert and *don't* reach for the check. The big question is what you will do *after* dinner.

The Lunch—To avoid the after-dinner dilemma, many gay men opt for a luncheon date. Since most of us are forced to work for a living, lunch is the ultimate safe sex date. You can tease and innuendo your way through your Caesar salad with impunity, knowing that a pile of work is waiting for you back at the office. If things get really hot, think how hot they'll be by the end of the day.

The Movie—A good choice. If you pick the right film (anything by Merchant & Ivory), you'll probably be one of dozens of gay couples in the theater. When the lights go down, will he put his hand on your knee? It may sound like a scene from *A Summer Place,* but it could be pretty romantic. And it has the added bonus of not requiring much conversation but giving you both something to discuss over espresso afterward.

The Gym—Don't be stupid. The only place performance anxiety is worse is the bedroom. You've got to realize that one of you will be able to bench-press more than the other. Don't injure yourself trying to prove otherwise. By the time a date at the gym is over, you're either embarrassed by your own performance or disheartened by his. And what about the showers?

The Weekend—Don't even *think* about it. Whether to the beach or the country, going away for the weekend together puts you both at a decided disadvantage. If it gets ugly, you're trapped. At least you'll get a close-up view of his personal hygiene habits, which may not be particularly appetizing. And of course there's that sticky question of sleeping arrangements. If the first date doesn't seem too early for all that, be prepared. Pack condoms.

" ...and to think that until he met me, Simon thought *The Ring Cycle* was a washer setting!"

MINDING YOUR P'S AND Q'S: ETIQUETTE FOR A ONE-NIGHT STAND

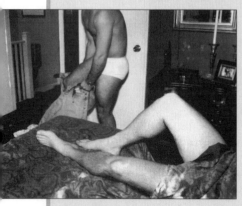

1. Be courteous to his roommate, cat, or other pet. Tell him how much you like his place, whether you do or not. (If you end up marrying him, *you* can do the decorating.)

2. If he offers you a drink or *other* treat, accept if he's having one. How well do you really know this guy anyway?

3. Search for signs of a lover when he leaves the room. If the same guy appears repeatedly in his pictures, it's acceptable (if not advisable) to ask who and *where* he is.

4. If, in the fluorescent light of his kitchen, you realize that his looks had been enhanced by the cosmetic effect of darkness at the bar, feign exhaustion and leave. One drink doesn't obligate you to do anything. You're not that cheap. Or are you?

5. Spend the night only if *he* invites you to. If he seems to be rushing you out the door, don't resist. He may have failed to mention that his lover is due home at any minute. Bow out gracefully. Don't beg.

6. If he offers breakfast in the morning, accept only if you're interested in seeing him again. Why should he slave over a hot stove when you won't remember his name by early afternoon? If he's really cute, offer to take him to brunch. Your friends will *hate* you.

7. While a thank-you note might be overdoing it, you probably owe him a call (or at least the courtesy of not ignoring him the next time you see him in public). But, *don't* call him the next day. You don't want to look that desperate.

8. Whatever you do, don't fall in love with him—at least not yet. There's a reason it's called a "one-night stand."

THE GOOD, THE BAD, AND THE UGLY: TELLING A WINNER FROM A LOSER

After the first date, a reasoned assessment of your new friend's long-term potential is in order. Occasionally, you realize before the entrée is even served that you never want to see the jerk again. But sometimes a fair evaluation takes a little time and a bit of reflection after the fact (or *act,* as the case may be). Because love is blind, there are certain *objective* questions you have to ask yourself.

INSTRUCTIONS: *Answer each of the following questions about your new romantic interest. Total the points provided for each question you answered "Yes." If he scores 30 points or less, go for it (he may be as good as it gets); between 30 and 60 points, it's a tough call—suggest a group activity for your next date (you can always slip away in the crowd); 60 points or higher, and you may want to consider getting an unlisted phone number.*

1. Did he check himself out every time he passed a mirror? *5 points.*

    A quick glance every once in a while is almost irresistible for any gay man, but if he spent more time using his soup spoon to check out his hair than looking at you, it's a problem.

2. If you went to a bar, did he seem to know everyone? *5 points.*

    It could be a sign that he's been around the block more than a few times. Of course, he may just have a lot of friends. If they're cute and/or really fun, subtract ten points from his final score.

3. Did he talk about himself incessantly? *10 points.*

    While the date may be painful, by the time it's over at least you'll know enough about him to know you're not interested in learning any more.

4. When the check came, did he suddenly remember that he "forgot" his wallet? *10 points.*

   Bad sign, unless you invited him, you've got money to burn, and/or he's cute enough to pay for. But don't fall for it; no one really *forgets his wallet.*

5. Did he refer to his ex-lover repeatedly? *15 points.*

   Don't let that rebound hit you in the face. Are you sure the lover is out of the picture, *or just out of* town?

6. Did he spend all evening discussing his relationship with his mother? *15 points.*

   You've got your own mother to deal with. And remember Norman Bates.

7. Did he start planning *your* schedule for the next month? *20 points.*

   Red alert! Unless it was love at first sight, you're probably not ready to decide where and with whom you'll be spending next Christmas.

8. At the end of the evening, did he insist on going to your place rather than his? *20 points.*

   What's he got to hide? Photos of him and his boyfriend all over the place? Or worse yet, a wife?

"Don't accept candy from strangers; get real estate."
   —BATHROOM GRAFFITI IN
   A NEW YORK HUSTLER BAR

PEST CONTROL:
GETTING RID OF UNWANTED TRICKS

Everyone has been guilty of a serious lapse in judgment at least once in his life. For those occasions, be prepared to cut your losses and end the evening before the First Act. Depending on how bad it is, and how much you care about your reputation, you can end it with either diplomacy or the cold, hard truth. Some suggestions:

1. You're not Mother Teresa. Be honest: "I'm sorry, there's been a terrible mistake."

2. Call him a cab and pay for it in advance.

3. Tell him how great it feels to be out on parole.

4. Ask him to help you find your bottle of Kwell.

5. Plan ahead. Use your ex's name instead of your own, and if you get cold feet before going home, give the would-be loverboy directions to your ex's house.

6. Tell him that your lover, a jealous linebacker with a bad temper, should be getting home any minute.

7. Pop *Basic Instinct* in the VCR and get out an ice pick.

8. Toss his wallet out a window. When he goes outside to get it, lock the door. Call the police.

9. On the other hand, when you finally get a trick, why would you want to get rid of him?

WHAT YOU SAY IS WHAT YOU GET: PHONE SEX PROTOCOL

"Gertrude Stein was right. A mouth is a mouth is a mouth."

—**RAY SHARKEY, IN** *SCENES FROM THE CLASS STRUGGLE IN BEVERLY HILLS*

In these days of technological miracles, you can now combine safe sex with home shopping. The telephone has become the gateway to a veritable pornucopia of options for sex-starved shut-ins. Giving a whole new meaning to "touch-tone phone," 976 numbers allow you to indulge your wildest fantasies without ever leaving your room or having to make someone breakfast in the morning. With 800 and 900 numbers, you can get intimate with men all over the country for a lot less than the airfare. You can choose prerecorded stories, voice mailboxes and bulletin boards on which to leave and retrieve messages, one-on-one talking, and the modern man's mating call, "chat lines." Sadly, reality often fails to live up to expectations.

Take the prerecorded "hot stories," advertised as true tales, told (of course) by "hot studs." Once you're on the hook for $3.00 per minute, you quickly realize that some guy with third-grade reading skills is struggling through a script that makes porn film dialogue sound like Proust. Once you get over your sympathy for the guy (who's making a fool of himself), you realize that you've spent five minutes ($15), and he's still on the warmup. The juicy details could be $5 to $10 dollars (or more) away. Embarrassed at your own desperation and concerned about your phone bill, you'll probably hang up before the story really gets interesting, *if* it ever does.

The next time, you might try a conference or "chat" line. If you do, you'll hear a group of other guys each trying to impress the others with the best, butchest "hello" he can muster. The hello-ing continues until someone takes the bait and indicates interest by following a "hello" with a "How ya' doin'?" or some other butch salutation in his best forced baritone. If you're interested in someone, speak up fast so no one else jumps ahead of you. The early bird gets the worm. And remember, you're paying by the minute.

Once you've connected with someone, electronic etiquette requires you both to rattle off a series of questions and answers in machine-gun fashion. "Whatdoyoulooklike?" [Answer] "Whatdo*you*looklike?" [Answer] "Howoldareyou?" [Answer] "Howoldare*you*?" [Answer] "Whatareyouinto?" [Answer] "Whatare*you*into?" [Answer]. After this exercise, you won't have a clue what the guy's *really* like, but unless you're planning to meet him ("hook up," in the language of lust), who cares?

Helpful Hint No. 1: Use a pseudonym. There are only a handful of acceptable names. It's amazing how often Jim, Tom, Dave, Pete, and Dirk phone in. If Ira, Edgar, and Herschel call, awkward silence. And Jim and his friends are all doctors, lawyers, or accountants. Some weekday afternoons, you may wonder who's saving the lives, trying the cases, and doing the books; all the doctors, lawyers, and accountants in town seem to be talking to each other on the chat lines. Gives the "old boy network" new meaning.

Helpful Hint No. 2: Embellish your answers. If you're five feet five, add six inches. If you're slightly overweight, say you have a "swimmer's body." Everyone expects you to stretch the truth a little. If you honestly say that you "have an average build" and are "decent-looking," everyone on the line will picture the Hunchback of Notre Dame. Awkward silence. If you *do* get the silent treatment, wait a moment. Soon the hello-ing will resume.

Helpful Hint No. 3: Watch out for guys who give out their phone numbers or, even worse, their addresses. These are the Phone Sluts, guys with calloused dialing fingers and all ten speed-dial buttons programmed for lust lines. They'll be the aggressive ones on the other end. If you call often enough, you'll be able to recognize their voices. Whatever you do, *don't give them your number,* or they won't leave you alone: You'll have your lover's parents over for a beautiful Christmas Eve dinner. The phone will ring. Your lover's dad answers it . . . "Hey, stud. You horny?" Awkward silence.

"Normal sex is still a novelty to most people."
    —AN EDITOR, *PRICK UP YOUR EARS*

HOW TO BREAK UP WITH A PSYCHO-KILLER

Not every guy takes rejection with dignity. Some can't handle it and may go off the deep end. Others live in the deep end. If you're dating a guy who loves to nibble on your ear and won't let you look in his freezer, chances are you'll eventually recognize the warning signs: He put sugar in the gas tank of a guy who snubbed him on the street, or he set his ex's bed on fire (with the ex in it) when they broke up. If so, you might want to consider a few survival tips when breaking up with him:

1. Do it in a well-lit, well-populated public place, either with friends nearby or surrounded by people you'll never see again. It could get ugly.

2. If you must do it at home, first hide all sharp objects and flammable materials.

3. Flatter him. Tell him he's too good for you. For once in your life, *try* to sound sincere.

4. Change the locks. Buy a home security system or a pit bull. Get Caller I.D.

5. Apply to the federal Witness Protection Program. Change your name. Move.

6. Fake your own death, and write a convincing obituary for the local paper.

7. Join a gang.

8. If all else fails, bring in the heavy artillery: Let your mother break the news to him. She's been waiting a lifetime for this opportunity.

CHAPTER VI
CATCHING THE BIG ONE
The Gay Couple

"I found Queequeg's arm thrown over me in the most loving and affectionate manner. You had almost thought I had been his wife . . . [H]e pressed his forehead against mine, clasped me round the waist, and said that henceforth we were married . . . Thus, then, in our hearts' honeymoon, lay I and Queequeg—a cosy, loving pair."

—ISHMAEL, IN HERMAN MELVILLE'S *MOBY-DICK*

Yes, Virginia, gay men really *can* find true love. (Whether they can remain monogamous is another question.)

Many gay men are skilled in the deep-sea fishing of dating and finally catch the Big One. Others just get fed up with the heartache and hassle of countless un-Happy Hours. (How much Whitney Houston can you stand?) They throw out a line and give commitment a chance, hoping at least for someone to do their laundry. So often, the one they catch has to be thrown back for being too small or any one of a million other reasons. For all those that got away, a lot of gay men eventually are caught hook, line, and sinker, and realize that commitment is not a four-letter word. In no time these newly domesticated guys find themselves happily arguing over fabric swatches for the ottoman in the den.

The gay couple is becoming increasingly common. Maybe the sexual Russian Roulette of the '80s has scared more guys into embarking on long-term relationships. Or maybe the gay couple is not a new phenomenon at all; perhaps the only thing changed is their ability to shop for a sleigh bed openly—at least in many parts of the country. In any event, gay couples are *very* "in." They are the quintessential DINKs (Dual Incomes, No Kids), who have advertisers, retailers, and fundraisers chomping at the bit. *Musts* on any guest list.

A GAY PSAT (PERSONALITY, SEXUALITY, AND TEMPERAMENT) EXAM FOR POTENTIAL FUTURE EX-LOVERS

Before you give out your number, much less start hyphenating your name with his, you'd better do a background check. Since there aren't Character Bureaus (like credit bureaus) to call when you meet someone, you need a basic aptitude test for potential significant others. The next time you meet someone you'd even *consider* dating, ask him to take this test:

Choose one answer to each question. Scoring is at the end.

1. When you were a kid, how did you get to school?
   a. *a big bus*
   b. *a little bus*
   c. *walked*
   d. *limousine*

2. How many boyfriends have you had in the past five years?
   a. *0*
   b. *1–10*
   c. *more than 10*
   d. *you lost count*

3. How many tricks have you had in the past five years?
   a. *0*
   b. *1–10*
   c. *more than 10*
   d. *you lost count*

4. How would you define the difference between a trick and a boyfriend?
   a. *Not applicable. You don't trick.*
   b. *A boyfriend is a trick you've seen three or more times.*
   c. *You know a boyfriend's name.*
   d. *A boyfriend agrees to have breakfast with you in the morning.*
   e. *There is no difference.*

5. At what point do you say, "I love you"?
   a. *after twenty minutes of making out*
   b. *after three dates*
   c. *only after at least three friends have graciously given their seal of approval*
   d. *Never. That would make you too vulnerable.*

6. What do you do for a living?
   a. *independently wealthy*
   b. *model or actor*
   c. *professional—lawyer, doctor, accountant*
   d. *unemployed*
   e. *other*

7. When you don't get your way with someone, you . . .
    a. try blackmail.
    b. besmirch his reputation.
    c. try to get the same thing from someone else.
    d. call home.

8. Complete the following sentence: People who commit violent crimes . . .
    a. must have a good reason for doing so.
    b. must have been mistreated as children.
    c. should be shot.
    d. should be punished as the law provides.

9. Complete the following sentence: The best part about having a boyfriend is . . .
    a. having someone to live for.
    b. always having something to do three-ways with.
    c. making your single friends jealous.
    d. nothing. It's too confining.

10. Complete the following sentence: The best part of moving in with someone is . . .
    a. moving out of your parents' home.
    b. having someone to do your laundry.
    c. being able to monitor his every move.
    d. when he goes out of town.

SCORING:

1. **a.** *or* **c.**—*He at least tends toward normal.* **b.**—*Check his medicine cabinet for Prozac or a similar drug.* **d.**—*He's either an insecure pathological liar or a hell of a good catch, at least financially.*

2. **a.**—*There's something seriously wrong; either he's too picky or there's a nasty side of him you haven't seen.* **b.**—*He's pretty normal.* **c.**— *Suggests someone with questionable standards who has to have a boyfriend at any cost.* **d.**—*He'll suck the life right out of you. Tell him to hit the road.*

3. **a.**—*He's either recently retired clergy, impotent, or hung-up sexually.* **b.**—*Indicates someone fairly selective but still willing to have a good time.* **c.**—*A sign of a healthy (perhaps over-active) libido; he could be lots of fun, if you can keep him interested.* **d.**—*He's trash and maybe trade: keep your eye on your wallet, and don't expect him to be there when you wake up.*

4. **a.**—*He won't sleep with you until you tell him you love him; is it really worth it? Possibly.* **b.**, **c.**, *or* **d.**—*He moves fast. Go to his place, and don't give him your phone number.* **e.**—*Steer clear of this one unless you're into co-dependence.*

5. **a.**—*He's either a desperado or a slut. Tell him you're married, and whatever you do, don't make out with him.* **b.**—*The guy hasn't had a boyfriend in a long time. He's an eager beaver, but not necessarily a loser.* **c.**—*He has no mind of his own. You can bet his friends are real charmers.* **d.**—*Ice princess. Unless you can do without emotional intimacy, you should look elsewhere.*

6. **a.**—*It's probably not true. He may be a drug dealer. In bars, do people swarm around him like bees to honey?* **b.**—*He's a waiter.* **c.**—*He's probably financially sound, but there's a risk he's somewhat (if not completely) boring, with boring friends.* **d.**—*He could be looking for a sugar daddy or at least a free place to crash. Caveat emptor.* **e.**—*If you're not looking to marry for money, be happy to find a guy with a steady job.*

7. **a.** *or* **b.**—*He's a vindictive little thing; watch out.* **c.**—*Give him credit for resourcefulness, but not for loyalty.* **d.**—*You have a spoiled boy on your hands; be prepared to discipline him.*

8. **a.**—*He's got a short fuse. Don't cross him.* **b.**—*This guy can rationalize anything; he's probably unreliable and irresponsible.* **c.**—*He's a right-wing fanatic, the kind of guy you may someday be tempted to poison (or emasculate).* **d.**—*He's fairly rational. Won't take any crap from you.*

9. **a.**—*Watch it; he'll smother you.* **b.**—*He'll be lots of fun if you don't care much about monogamy. Check for STDs.* **c.**—*This is the type that runs a credit check on you before agreeing to go out. If you don't drive a flashy car, forget it.* **d.**—*He's terrified of commitment, set in his ways—a loner.*

10. **a.**—*He's either a mama's boy, unemployed, or jail bait.* **b.**—*He's looking for a* hausfrau, *not a boyfriend.* **c.**—*Living with him would be like living with J. Edgar Hoover.* **d.**—*You can take the girl out of the bars, but you can't take the bars out of the girl.*

HOW TO TELL HE'S THE ONE

Okay, so you've dated, you've danced, and you've dallied. You've finally found someone who did better than a D– on your screening exam. But how do you know if you've struck pay dirt? Some say you just know. But how? For those who aren't that adept at reading tea leaves, or don't even *drink* tea (it *does* stain your teeth), here are a few signs that he's Mr. Right:

1. You put his number on your speed dial at work.

2. You don't mind that he and your secretary or co-workers have become chummy.

3. You have an uncontrollable urge to kiss him in elevators.

4. Your friends start to call *him* directly.

5. Your closet is losing the battle against his clothes.

6. You use his name regularly with your parents.

7. You find excuses to call him at all hours.

8. You share the same sweater size, and he has beautiful sweaters.

MERGERS AND ACQUISITIONS: MOVING IN TOGETHER

"Gay liberation should not be a license to be a
perpetual adolescent. If you deny yourself commitment,
then what can you do with your life?"
—HARVEY FIERSTEIN, IN *TORCH SONG TRILOGY*

Embarking on a committed relationship may seem like a big step, but it's a small one compared to the giant leap of moving in together. Cohabiting (particularly in a one-room or one-bedroom apartment) confirms the world's suspicions that the two of you are more than good friends. Few thrills can match the look on an appliance repairman's face when he is is greeted at the door by two men in pajamas. But realtors' eyes *do* light up when two men, obviously having disposable dollars and no dependents, announce that they're house hunting together. It's all just part of married life.

Of course, living together isn't for everyone. Some guys would rather be committed than find themselves in a committed relationship. They may get all the companionship they need from a dog, a cat, or the *Dieffenbachia* in their living room. But for those who like the warmth of another mammal in bed next to them and don't want fleas, nothing provides the constant comfort they seek like living with a lover. Still, a word of advice to these guys: Look before jumping off lovers' leap.

" ...it wasn't enough that
we had to name the dogs
Lorna and Liza,
but ringing bells on a damn
trolley in St. Louis
worked my last nerve!"

SIX THINGS YOU'LL WISH YOU'D THOUGHT OF WHEN IT'S TOO LATE

Living together is not something to rush into without serious thought and careful planning. It may not be possible to merge two impeccable, but different, tastes into one home. Will your Biedermeier chairs go with his Donghia dining room table? Don't even think about it. You know how people talk. But interior design is just one of a number of issues to consider:

1. When you move in together, it'll no longer be just Jim, but Jim-and-Lee, and not just Warren, but Warren-and-Ben. And you thought you were getting a live-in lover, not a Siamese twin.

2. You're splitting the cost of every new home furnishing he says is an absolute must. In case things ever go sour, make sure you have some claim to that booty. Half a coffee table won't do either of you any good; the only thing you'll ever need with two legs is another man.

3. You're an anti-smoker dating the Marlboro man. Knowing that he smokes an occasional cigarette is a far cry from having to smell it on your clothes or in bed next to you.

4. Your fragile ego can't stand the fact that he makes more money than you. Learn to make the most of it. If you have to sweep an issue or two under the rug, isn't a Persian better than a dhurrie?

5. You don't share his view of monogamy or vice versa. Don't rush to unpack your things or hang your botanical prints. You may be moving sooner than you think.

6. He's not out to his parents, and their frequent visits mean you constantly have to de-gay your place and sleep on the sofabed. If they insist on clinging to the absurd notion that two single thirty-five-year-old guys living together just haven't found the right girl, it's not *your* place to set them straight. But make *him* sleep on the sofabed.

"...and *please* let Bruce and Mitchell figure out what we need around here is a *real* bitch."

THE TIES THAT BIND:
MORTGAGES AND OTHER FORMS OF BONDAGE

A mortgage can prove to be a much stronger bond than any marriage license. And the more material possessions a couple owns jointly, the more inextricably bound together they find themselves. Not an insignificant consideration when you consider that many guppie couples own not only their primary residence together, but a weekend getaway. Gay couples often buy their cars together, too, and most, if not all, of their other big-ticket items—stereos, TVs, couches, rugs, tanning beds. Each jointly-owned possession is just one more knot in the ties that bind.

Is that so bad? For those who really value a committed relationship, but sometimes need a little incentive to keep them from running off with the hunk they met at the grocery store, mortgages and other forms of material bondage serve a valuable purpose. The mere thought of the bloodbath involved in dividing the joint possessions (or the horror of losing any of them) is enough to make you rethink that fantasy and decline the hunk's tempting proposition.

If you really love each other, don't be afraid of committing yourselves to some major joint investment. Dealing with the bank may feel a little awkward at first, but they've seen it before. They *love* customers like you. So go for it. You'll be glad to have that mortgage when your other half comes home with groceries in his arms and some hunk on his mind.

ALWAYS A BRIDESMAID . . . ADVICE ON GAY WEDDINGS

"Why would a guy want to marry a guy?"
"Security."

—TONY CURTIS AND JACK LEMMON,
IN *SOME LIKE IT HOT*

More and more gay couples are formalizing their relationships with a wedding or commitment ceremony (usually not the kind that involves a psychiatric institution). These ceremonies can range from simple (a few barefooted friends on the beach singing "Kumbayah") to ostentatious (a few hundred of your closest friends in black tie at the Plaza with Lester Lanin's Orchestra). To cynics, these ceremonies are only excuses for throwing a party and getting gifts. So what? Our straight friends have been milking everyone for china and stemware for years; why can't we?

If you decide to have a commitment ceremony, you'll need to determine whether it will be secular or religious. Most guys choose religious. As long as you're going to give your parents palpitations, you might as well go for cardiac arrest. Lutherans Concerned actually has a ceremony for gay couples called the "Ceremony of the Three Cups." It begins with drinking from the Cup of Bitterness, moves on to a gulp from the Cup of Sweetness, and concludes with a sip from the Cup of Salvation. Of course, if things go sour, you'll probably come full circle and be swilling from the Cup of Bitterness by the time it's all over.

Many guys find the whole ceremony thing a bit much for their taste. For some of these, merely exchanging rings provides as much of a symbolic statement as they're ready to make. Of course, there is *the* gay wedding ring. Sometimes known as a Turkish or Russian wedding ring, it consists of three interlocking bands of gold, silver, or platinum. In the case of the Cartier "rolling ring," yellow, rose, and white gold. *Très cher.* Worn like a wedding ring, but *always* on the right hand. (If your lights just dimmed, it's because of all the lightbulbs going on in the heads of straight readers.)

The only problem with a simple exchange of rings is that, without a ceremony, you miss out on two of the best parts of weddings: the reception and the gifts. Gay wedding receptions can be some of the most glamorous and/or enjoyable social events of the year. With all those friends and lovers in catering or the restaurant business, are you surprised? If the relationship fizzles, at least everyone will remember the party. And who couldn't use a new blender?

"What do you think happens when we die?"
"We get to have sex again."
—STEPHEN CAFFREY AND CAMPBELL SCOTT, IN
LONGTIME COMPANION

THINGS TO CONSIDER WHEN PLANNING A GAY WEDDING

Who gets to throw the bouquet?

Whose friend gets to make the bouquet?

Does one of you get to wear a wedding dress? If you both want to, why let tradition stand in the way?

Can either of you honestly wear white?

Do you both get to pick a best man or maid of honor, as the case may be?

Is it gauche if you've slept with either one of them?

Is peach a flattering color for your bridesmaids?

What do you call your bridesmaids?

What song will you choose for your first dance? "Crucified"?

Who gets the bachelor party? (More importantly, who's the "entertainment" at the bachelor party?)

Do you need a trousseau? *(Of course.)*

Where should you go on your honeymoon? (See Chapter VII.)

KEEPING THE HOME FIRES BURNING WITHOUT GETTING SCORCHED

> "To keep a relationship fresh, think of it as a series of one-night stands."
>
> **—DAVID B. FEINBERG, IN *EIGHTY-SIXED***

With six out of ten straight marriages ending in divorce, it should be no surprise that gay couples, too, confront their share of bumps along the road. The obstacles to a successful gay relationship at times seem formidable. Issues of money, career, family, or the mere proximity of two adult men under one roof provide enough pyrotechnics for a pretty colorful fireworks show. How do you keep the home fires burning without getting scorched? Different approaches work for different couples, but there are a few favorites:

Pets: Most gay men are childless. As a result, there are a lot of guys out there with unfulfilled paternal instincts. (Some of us, on the other hand, get a nervous twitch whenever we're around kids for more than an hour.) For those in a relationship, this lack of fulfillment can be compounded by the need for something—anything—to keep things interesting. Often the solution comes with four legs and more body hair than the two of you combined. Be it a dog, cat, some rare birds, or even a tank of tropical fish, pets provide a male couple with the children they don't, and may never, have. Something for them to love that will return that love unconditionally—unlike their lover.

Without endorsing one option over another, a dog may be the gay couple's best friend. (Fish may not love you back, birds are messy, and a cat may be the only creature bitchier than you.) Instead of arguing over really important issues—like the fact that you haven't had sex in five months—you can fight over who takes Fido out in the morning. And with the right clothes and the proper breed (*and* proper dog name, e.g., Jackson, Chauncey, or Brie), a dog may be your best accessory. If the relationship sours, the pooch could prove to be a great way to meet someone new—another dog lover, of course.

The Flavor of the Month: He fills a void in gay relationships much the way a pet might, but the flavor of the month doesn't require any litter boxes or leashes—usually. Not pistachio, though sometimes a dip, the flavor of the month is another guy who becomes the focal point of the gay couple's attention. It's not a sexual thing, although sex has more than likely crossed the minds of at least one (if not all three) of the players involved. Rather, the couple all but adopts their newfound friend, making sure he's well-fed, well-clothed, and *always* by their side.

Being chosen as the flavor of the month certainly has its advantages. There are a lot of single guys starving for that kind of attention, not to mention the home-cooked meals. And strong friendships often do develop. But being the flavor of the month is by definition a temporary thing. The couple decides they need to spend an evening or two alone. Or the flavor finds a boyfriend and no longer needs the couple's caretaking. More often than not, he eventually sees his special status usurped by a younger, cuter, more needy fellow. Baskin-Robbins and its thirty-one have nothing on couples who've stayed together for years using this technique.

"I can resist anything but temptation."

—OSCAR WILDE

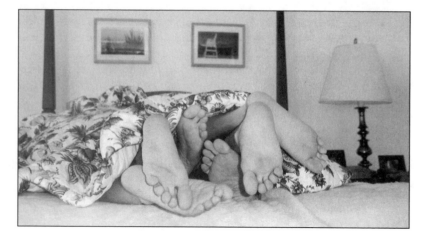

2 + 1 and Other Sexual Mathematics: Straight or gay, a lifetime of monogamy is easier in theory than in practice. Affairs of the heart are often just that—*affairs*—and gay couples are no different than anybody else. Sex (if they're even having it) with the same man for years can become a bit rote, or as Merriam-Webster defines it, a "routine or repetition carried out mechanically or unthinkingly." Not quite the stuff fantasies are made of. All gay couples, at one time or another, find themselves searching for something to turn up the heat in the bedroom. Some turn to self-help books, seminars, and counseling; others opt to "open" their relationship.

An "open" relationship defies definition. Theoretically, it could involve as many possible combinations as the Lotto, but should *always* include a condom or two. For couples just learning this new kind of sexual algebra, the three-way (that's 2 + 1) may be the easiest equation. Seeing your lover with another may be enough to make you realize just how attractive he really is. But these sexual mathematics may be a bit disconcerting, particularly if the new addition and your lover aren't paying any attention to *you*. Some couples attempt a more advanced calculus and decide to give each other complete sexual freedom. (That's $(a + b) + c + d = (a + c)$ and $(b + d)$.) A couple of forty-year-olds may each go off searching for a younger man. After all, twenty goes into forty twice as many times as forty does. But take care in trying to multiply your pleasure in this way or you and your lover may end up in 2 single beds divided by 1 nightstand.

Spending Your Way to Happiness: The power of positive spending should not be undervalued when it comes to looking for ways to protect the investment in your relationship. The '80s may be over, but excessive material acquisition continues to thrive in many gay households. An antique Oriental, a BMW, or a beach house can add more to a gay couple's equity than to their net worth. Marriage can sometimes be rough, but when the going gets tough, the tough go shopping. If you're both feeling ambivalent toward your relationship, simple acquisitions such as Pratesi bedding, a multiple CD player, or a food processor may lift you out of the doldrums. If the winter of your discontent is particularly harsh, you may need an antique or an original piece of art to relight the fire.

Besides the obvious impact on your checking account (or more likely your credit card balance), spending your way to happiness can be woefully fleeting in its restorative effects on your relationship. In a matter of weeks, some dizzy queen may drop an ash on your new rug, and as it burns a hole in it, your *own* newfound spark will fade. Depending on your bank balance or credit limit (and the size of your house), you may again find yourselves in the market for some new trinket or toy to improve your relationship's balance sheet. If you're not careful, this vicious spending cycle could bankrupt the two of you, if not your relationship.

MOMMIE DEAREST:
HOW TO AVOID KILLING YOUR LOVER'S MOTHER

The worst TV antics of Eve Arden and Kaye Ballard pale in comparison to the machinations of *his* beloved mother. Whether she's the Donna Reed type or some combination of Bette Davis and Cruella De Vil, admit it: Homicide has crossed your mind. If it's not the fact that you're not the girl next door, it's your career, your clothes, your cooking, or your penchant for Lladro. Whatever it is, her son is a "darling boy"; *you're* the gay one. How can you keep from strangling the woman? It isn't easy, but give the following techniques a try:

1. Consider *his* relationship with *your* mother. It's probably no cachepot of potpourri either. Besides, she's the only mother he's got.

2. Screen all calls; you could go for months without speaking to her.

3. Beware the Trojan Horse phenomenon. Any gifts she gives may have more than apron strings attached; that horrible sweater from three birthdays ago could be pulled out and thrown in your face at a moment's notice.

4. Suggest that you and your lover go to the islands for the holidays or celebrate them on some other neutral ground. The temptation to put arsenic in her eggnog may be irresistible.

5. If all else fails, move to the opposite coast. A murder trial may be one of your finest dramatic moments, but those orange prison jumpsuits won't do a thing for you.

SPLITTING HAIRS:
DIVORCE AND DIVIDING THE BOOTY

"I gave him my youth!"

—ROSALIND RUSSELL, IN *THE WOMEN*

Regrettably, not every relationship can withstand the test of time (or temptation). Eventually the day may come when you find yourself singing along with Tammy Wynette's D-I-V-O-R-C-E. With no court or lawyers involved, and without the benefit of community property laws, splitting up sends gay couples into a veritable tailspin of "what's mine is mine, and what's yours is mine." If you thought Lorena went for the family jewels, you ain't seen nothing. After years (or months) of acquiring tasteful possessions as a couple, you are suddenly faced with dividing the booty. Will one of you keep the house? Who will get the Bang & Olufsen stereo? What about the yellow Lab? You may want to hire a mediator—or a referee.

Material possessions aside, one of the most unfortunate aspects of a gay couple's breakup is the impact it has on their circle of friends. With children typically absent from the picture, gay men and their friends truly become an extension of, if not replacement for, each other's family. Like the breakup of a husband and wife, a gay couple's divorce sends shockwaves throughout that family, or at least sets their phone lines buzzing. Some of your friends may feel compelled to take sides. A bit of advice: As your relationship crashes and burns, do your best not to take your friends down with you. When all is said and done, you may want to date one of them. Don't let them see you at your darkest hour. Divorce him with dignity.

With that out of the way, who gets the Waterford?

CHAPTER VII

LIVING THE DIAMOND LIFE IN A RHINESTONE WORLD
Gay Culture

"I don't think there is a 'gay lifestyle.' I think that's superficial crap, all that talk about gay culture. A couple of restaurants on Castro Street and a couple of magazines do not constitute culture. Michelangelo is culture. Virginia Woolf is culture. So let's don't confuse our terms. Wearing earrings is not culture..."

—RITA MAE BROWN

There comes a time when every gay man realizes that life is *not* a Polo ad. Still, that doesn't stop him from trying to make it so.

Whether or not they succeed in personifying Madison Avenue's vision of the good life, gay men possess a *joie de vivre* that many others don't. Be it an intimate dinner for thirty or a raft race down the Chattahoochee River, gay men do it with unsurpassed style. From dining out and dancing to vacationing and entertaining, gay men lead a lifestyle that would make even Ivana blink.

That's not to say that gay culture is nothing more than living well *or* that the pursuit of pleasure is the *only* thing on gay men's minds. Consider the unparalleled gay contributions to art, music, literature, and the artificial tanning industry. Most importantly, when faced with a disease of epic proportions, gay men have answered the call and taken volunteerism to new heights. (In doing so, they've set new standards for event planning—the fundraisers can be *fabulous*.) With all this and a knack for *creating* (rather than just *spotting*) trends, it might seem that "gay culture" is redundant. Sorry, Rita Mae. Gay = culture.

"O.K. now, splash on that cheap cologne, put on the Anita Bryant tape, *and let's Polka!*"

Gay Hell

SATURDAY NIGHT AT THE MOVIES: EIGHTEEN FILMS EVERY GAY MAN SHOULD SEE

"Is that pornography or art?"

"If it's in focus, it's pornography. If it's out of focus, it's art."
—**MICHAEL MURPHY AND LINDA HUNT,**
IN THE YEAR OF LIVING DANGEROUSLY

Hollywood's influence over gay men—and vice versa—cannot be overestimated. What with sirens like Bette Davis, Joan Crawford, and Charles Nelson Reilly, it's easy to understand the fascination of gay men with the silver screen. Besides providing reams of material for budding drag queens, the movies portray a world in which every gay man, perhaps subconsciously, wishes to live—the men are gorgeous and the gowns glamorous. With that in mind, paring down the must-see list of films to under twenty isn't easy—Gym Dandies may insist on *Pumping Iron* while A-Listers demand *The Philadelphia Story*. Recognizing the imperfection of the science, here are eighteen that every gay man should see:

1. **All About Eve**—With so many fabulous Bette Davis movies, it's almost impossible to pick only one as a must-see. In this one, she plays the fabled Margo Channing, a middle-aged Broadway actress who makes the same mistake Adam did—trusting Eve. One of the all-time great lines in cinematic history is in this film. Which one? Rent it and see.

2. **Another Country**—What really goes on in those bastions of privilege, English boarding schools? This film will confirm your suspicions. After betraying his homeland, Guy Bennett reminisces on how he flaunted his love for his prep school classmates. Perhaps visually the most beautiful film on the list (Rupert Everett isn't exactly

chopped liver), the costumes triggered a gay obsession with the English country look, making Ralph Lauren a *very* rich man.

3. **The Boys in the Band**—This film makes the list not because it was Hollywood's first in which every major character is gay, but rather as a time capsule of an era that has fortunately gone by. With lines like "You show me a happy homosexual, and I'll show you a gay corpse," you'll gain a new appreciation for just how far we've come.

4. **Cabaret**—Bob Fosse's film version of the Broadway musical based on Christopher Isherwood's *Goodbye to Berlin.* Michael York plays a bisexual British student living in Berlin in the carefree pre-Nazi '30s. He's sleeping with Liza Minnelli, who plays a torch singer at a gender-bending cabaret; eventually they discover that they're both sleeping with the same man. It made Liza a star, but now it's time for her to find a new gig.

5. **Gentlemen Prefer Blondes**—This quintessential '50s Hollywood musical is timeless. Marilyn Monroe, with the help of her sidekick Jane Russell, sets out to marry a millionaire and ends up crossing the Atlantic with the U.S. Olympic team. Great musical numbers taking full advantage of the beefcake on board. It's this flick in which Marilyn shows Madonna why "Diamonds Are a Girl's Best Friend."

6. **Hairspray**—Every list of favorite gay films should include at least one John Waters/Divine collaboration. This one is the least likely to turn your stomach. Waters casts Divine as the proud mother of Ricki Lake (before she became a TV talking head) who shows the Baltimore of 1963 the virtues of high hair and racial integration. Great cameo by gay diva Deborah Harry.

7. **La Cage aux Folles**—A couple of middle-aged lovers, Renato owns a nightclub where Albin (aka Zaza) is the star attraction. All's well until Renato's son brings home

his fiancée and her conservative parents to meet his father and "mother." One of the highest-grossing foreign films of all time, this French farce brought drag to the masses and they loved it.

8. **Longtime Companion**—A small circle of friends confronts AIDS and watches their circle grow smaller in its wake. The first major motion picture to address AIDS head-on and cross over to a "mainstream"—whatever that means—audience. Bruce Davison got the Oscar nomination, but Stephen Caffrey takes the prize for his true-to-life portrayal of a gay man lip-synching "Dreamgirls" in the privacy of his own home.

9. **Mommie Dearest**—How dare that ungrateful Christina do this to Joan! A not-very-pretty portrayal of Joan Crawford's sado-maternal instincts, this piece of familial character assassination is a classic for the exaggerated, unbridled cruelty of its title character. You'll think twice before using wire hangers again.

10. **My Beautiful Laundrette**—Tough guy Johnny helps Omar, his Pakistani boyfriend, turn a trick and a profit in the coin laundry business. Years before Daniel Day-Lewis won the Oscar, he stole many a gay man's heart as the British punk who crossed racial and sexual lines for love and clean underwear.

11. **Paris Is Burning**—For those who don't live in New York, this documentary about African-American drag queens competing in "balls" and voguing contests may be a real eye-opener. We're not all WASPy types with gym memberships—thank God. This film celebrates our diversity and sets the record straight on who invented voguing; it *wasn't* Madonna.

12. **A Streetcar Named Desire**—When you read the Tennessee Williams classic in high school, you probably didn't picture the sensuality of this 1951 screen adaptation (or at least not the bulging muscles of hot young Marlon Brando). Vivien Leigh depends on the

"kindness of strangers" to make it through the day. What gay man would argue with that?

13. **Sunset Boulevard**—Long before Andrew Lloyd Weber got involved, Gloria Swanson was ready for her closeup in this '50s classic of a fading star grasping for the last rays of youth through the eyes of hunky William Holden. A parable for those aging queens who think a twentysomething boyfriend may be their fountain of youth.

14. **The Times of Harvey Milk**—The Oscar-winning documentary recounting the life of Harvey Milk, the openly gay San Francisco City Supervisor who, along with Mayor George Moscone, was assassinated in 1978. Milk was a symbol of the emerging gay political clout in the years after Stonewall. This film is a powerful tribute to a man who made a difference.

15. **What Ever Happened to Baby Jane?**—In this camp classic, Bette Davis and Joan Crawford play a pair of tragic sisters forced by circumstances to grow old together, proving that familiarity really does breed contempt. Bette's musical rendition of "I've Written a Letter to Daddy" (with Shirley Temple drag and baby-face makeup to boot) may be one of the all-time campiest scenes in film history.

16. **The Wizard of Oz**—Okay, it's pretty predictable, but at least you'll be able to understand all the Judy Garland and Yellow Brick Road references made around the piano bar. It's been described as an allegory for gay men fleeing the drab (i.e., black-and-white) world to a Technicolor fantasyland over the rainbow.

17. **The Women**—The kid gloves come off and the claws come out in this all-female movie written by women. Clare Boothe Luce strikes a chord with this biting satire of the mores and machinations of high society dames. And *you* thought *your* friends were bitchy. Advertised as "135 women with men on their minds," this film is

quoted in some gay circles as often as fundamentalists quote scripture.

18. **Women in Love**—Based on D. H. Lawrence's classic story of repressed sexuality, this film gets the nod as the most sensual on the list. Unable to satisfy his needs with the women in his life, Gerald resists the attraction he feels to his friend Rupert. Instead of sex, they wrestle in the nude; this scene alone makes the movie a must.

"I *am* big! It's the pictures that got small!"
—**GLORIA SWANSON, IN *SUNSET BOULEVARD***

TEN SKILLS EVERY GAY MAN SHOULD MASTER

1. Listening to others. (It may be difficult, but at least try. The best way to make someone comfortable is *not* to talk about *yourself*, but to let *him* talk about *himself*.)

2. Playing one sport reasonably well. (Whether it's golf or badminton, knowing the rules of at least one sport will come in handy. Besides, an affinity for one sport—be it tennis, skiing, or riding—has incredible wardrobe potential.)

3. Mixing at least three kinds of cocktails. (You need to ask why?)

4. Preparing one good meal. (And that doesn't mean a recipe requiring Cheez Wiz, but something you can serve to dinner guests that won't make them gag.)

5. Knowing the proper pronunciation and spelling of important French words *(Moët, je ne sais quois,* and *n'est-ce pas)* or at least being fluent in "menu French."

6. Writing a proper thank-you note. (Essential if you ever want to get invited anywhere again.)

7. Engaging in, or at least understanding, witty conversation. (If you're really cute, this may not matter—not much does. If you're not, it's critical.)

8. Tying a bow tie. (A real bow tie can be a subtle signal to other *boys* that you, too, appreciate the finer things.)

9. Being able to do something artistic and with flair, whether it's playing a musical instrument, decorating a room, wrapping a present, or even putting an outfit together. (Don't let that God-given talent go to waste. We *do* have our reputations to maintain.)

10. Putting on a condom. (Celibacy isn't necessary; good sense is.)

ASK BOUGAINVILLEA:

Gay Etiquette & Other Trivia

Dear Bougainvillea,

I recently started dating somebody new. Everything has been going great, but I've just learned that one of his best friends is someone I had a one-night stand with a few months ago. My boyfriend has been pushing for the three of us to have dinner so that this other guy can "meet" me. What should I do? I really like my new beau and am hoping things work out with him. I don't want him to think I'm some kind of whore.

Worried in Wisconsin.

Dear Worried,

Don't be. You're not the first girl to find herself between a rock and a hard place. Consider yourself lucky. A hard place is good to find. Unless you met your new man in a monastery, *his* past may be even darker than *yours*. And, girlfriend, one tryst does not a whore make, take it from *moi*. Honey, these days a boyfriend's sexual history should be one of the first things you both talk about. Tell loverboy up front, *before* any dinner reservations are made. If he's the prince charming you say he is (and trust Bougainvillea—they never are), he'll get over it. Besides, what if you're not as memorable as you think, and his friend has forgotten your name or, worse, the entire tawdry episode? As much as I love a good catfight, avoid an awkward, embarrassing scene at the restaurant. Remember Bougainvillea's first rule for gay romance: Strike early, strike often.

Dear Bougainvillea,

A really cute guy just started working in my office, and I'm pretty sure he's gay. The trouble is he keeps to himself and I sense that he's not all that comfortable with his sexuality. I could use a comrade at work and would like to get to know him better. What can I do to let him know I'm gay and make him feel more at ease?

Working It in West Hollywood

Dear Working Girl,

Are you looking for a buddy or a boyfriend? Either way, you're walking a thin line, Mary. What if he's not gay? Bougainvillea has it on the best authority that there are a few good-looking straight men out there . . . somewhere. Find some legitimate work-related reason to get to know him (that *doesn't* include massaging his aching shoulders at the end of the day). Sooner or later, he'll get used to you following him into the men's room. You'll be able to start dropping those telltale hints—mentioning an article you saw in last month's *Vanity Fair*, asking him where he got his tan, or discussing Hillary Clinton's hair. If he turns out to be gay and you can't keep it in your pants, watch out. You'll have a tough time trying to explain to the rest of the office why he hurled a tape dispenser at you. Given their pitfalls, Bougainvillea has always frowned on office romances. As Bougainvillea always says, keep your trash where it belongs—in the bedroom, not the boardroom.

Dear Bougainvillea,

Two close friends of mine who have been together for years recently decided to call it quits. It's for the best, but the split has been less than amicable. I've always been very attracted to one of them and would like to pursue more than a friendship with him. How long should I wait to make a move so I don't alienate my other friend, his ex?

Faithful Friend in Falmouth

Dear 'Mouth,

A *long* time. With friends like you, who needs mothers-in-law? If the divorce was nasty, you'll be lucky if you're able to maintain a *friendship* with both, let alone a *romance* with one. Still, Bougainvillea knows well that boys will be boys. (Oh, how she knows.) If you must pursue this stud—as if there aren't any other bulls in the pen—be prepared to lose what flimsy friendship you obviously have with the other. Hell hath no fury like an ex-lover's scorn. To put it bluntly, if you did it to Bougainvillea, she'd scratch your eyes out.

Dear Bougainvillea,

I'm in my early thirties and I just returned from vacation, where I met the most incredible guy. The only problem is, I live in Ohio and he lives in Orlando. I think he could be the one, but neither of us wants to move. We can only afford to see each other every three months. Between visits, should I not see other people? The winters can get pretty cold here.

Climbing the Walls in Cleveland

Dear Wallflower,

Bougainvillea always says, "Don't let a juicy fruit wither on the vine." Time and Bougainvillea wait for no man. Your situation sounds pretty clear-cut. If neither of you is willing to move, your relationship is going nowhere fast. Why torture yourselves? Honey, you're not getting any younger. You both owe it to yourselves to field a player from the hometown team. Speaking of which, where in Orlando does this hunk live?

TIGHT ENDS AND OTHER REASONS GAYS LOVE SPORTS

Some people suffer under the delusion that gay men are all limp-wristed sissies who throw like girls. (These are the same people who think it's great for football players to hug and pat each other on the butt, but point fingers and name-call when two guys do it on the street.) They've obviously never heard of the Gay Games, the Front Runners, or the International Gay Rodeo Association. And they must not have set foot in a gym in years.

Many gay men are talented, natural athletes, whose coordination, strength, and powers of concentration make them as good or better competitors than their straight counterparts. Anyone who thinks that gays lack a competitive spirit has never been to a Barneys warehouse sale (or any other endeavor, for that matter; gay men *always* have to be number one). And you can't go to a gym anymore without running into at least a few brethren who return your knowing glances. The gayer the gym, the better the bodies—and the more intimidating. From New York's Better Bodies ("Bitter Beauties") to D.C.'s Washington Sports ("Spa Lady") or West Hollywood's Sports Connection ("Sports Erection"), the all- or mostly-gay gym is an aesthetic experience every gay man should witness at least once. If you're not in tip-top shape, however, consider wearing a muumuu instead of a tank top.

Although gay men consistently are among the top competitors in the leading bodybuilding contests, not every gay man wants to look like Bob Jackson-Paris, the gay god of bodybuilding. (Okay, so we all do, but we're either too lazy or, alas, genetically deprived.) A lot of guys opt for sleeker runners' builds over beefy bulk. For these men, there are the Front Runners and other gay running organizations, located in at least sixteen states and the District of Columbia. Joining one of these groups isn't only good for your physical fitness, it can also be great for your social life. If you can't figure out whether a running club is primarily gay, wait for a competition; if the guys insist on seeing the T-shirt from the race before signing up, it's a gay group.

SEE STEPHEN RUN; RUN STEPHEN RUN— THE FRONT RUNNERS

You can find the Front Runners or similar gay running organizations in the following cities, and maybe others:

Tucson, AZ	Berkeley, CA	Long Beach, CA
San Diego, CA	San Francisco, CA	Santa Monica, CA
Denver, CO	Washington, DC	Ft. Lauderdale, FL
Chicago, IL	Louisville, KY	Baltimore, MD
Boston, MA	Minneapolis, MN	Kansas City, MO
New York, NY	Eugene, OR	Portland, OR
Philadelphia, PA	Houston, TX	San Antonio, TX
Seattle, WA		

For those who love the great outdoors, but don't care to run, there are gay outdoors organizations (both athletic and otherwise) in a number of cities. These groups sponsor outings for everything from bird-watching and biking to hiking and camping. If you're the type that likes to go down (downhill, that is), join a gay ski club. And virtually every city has gay bowling leagues, softball leagues, and, in some cases, even swim teams. To find the leagues in your area, pick up a copy of the local gay paper. Stop complaining about never meeting the right guys: Get out of the bars and onto the softball field.

THE GAY GAMES

One of the crowning athletic achievements of the modern gay world is the Gay Games, Olympics-like competitions for gay men and lesbians. Sponsored by the Federation of Gay Games, the Games include athletic competitions as well as a cultural festival. Gay Games IV, held in New York City in 1994, included over 10,000 participants from over three hundred cities, states, and countries.

The Gay Games offer something for everyone with an interest in sports. Events include:

Aerobics	Badminton	Billiards
Bowling	Cycling	Diving
Figure Skating	Flag Football	Golf
Ice Hockey	In-Line Skating	Judo
Martial Arts	Physique	Powerlifting
Racquetball	Soccer	Softball
Sport Climbing	Squash	Swimming
Table Tennis	Tennis	Track & Field
Volleyball	Water Polo	Wrestling

Athletes and artists interested in participating in the next Gay Games should contact the Federation of Gay Games, 584 Castro Street, Suite 343, San Francisco, California 94114, or their local Gay Games coordinating committee.

TIE ME UP, TIE ME DOWN:
THE GAY RODEO

"Don't fuck with me, fellas—this ain't my first time at the rodeo."

—FAYE DUNAWAY, IN *MOMMIE DEAREST*

One of the many examples of how gay men defy stereotyping is the Gay Rodeo. Leave it to gay men to devise a way to live out a childhood fantasy of life on the all-male Ponderosa while combining traditional butch rodeo events with spectacular camp drag. Started in 1975, Gay Rodeos are sponsored by the International Gay Rodeo Association (IGRA). Each year a dozen or so Gay Rodeos are held in various locales, most west of the Mississippi. With as many as fifteen thousand fans attending, you can imagine that they're happy hunting grounds for guys looking for something other than a cow to poke.

Both men and women participate. (Anyone who thinks women don't belong in combat should take in a lesbian rodeo event.) Events include Bareback Bronc Riding, Breakaway Calf Roping, Wild Bull Riding, and Barrel Chasing. Camp events include Steer Decorating, Wild Drag Racing, and Pole Bending (don't ask). Cash prizes are awarded to the winners. The losers don't sit down for a week. Less adventurous guys can usually find food, souvenirs, and dancing (Texas two-step, square dancing, and clogging, of course), and enough Tammy Wynette, Dolly Parton, and Patsy Cline look-alikes to fill the Grand Ol' Opry.

If your idea of a good time includes a bullwhip and spurs, or if you just like the way a pair of cowboy boots lifts your sagging derrière, check out a Gay Rodeo. For more information, call the IGRA Hotline at (303) 832-4472.

BLOW, GABRIEL, BLOW: GAY BANDS AND CHORUSES

"What's better than roses on your piano?"
"Tulips on your organ."

Two of the favorite non-athletic pastimes of gay men are
singing in a gay chorus and playing in a gay and lesbian band.
Gay men's choruses provide social outlets of note in over
twenty-six states and the District of Columbia. It's remarkable
what they can do without altos and sopranos. Gay and lesbian
bands make beautiful music together in over fourteen states
and the nation's capital.

Like everything else gay men tackle, chorus and band are
serious pursuits, not for *dilettantes*. Anyone who's witnessed
the resoluteness with which the sequin-clad drum majors and
baton twirlers (male, of course) lead the gay and lesbian bands
in Gay Pride parades knows this. But it's not just Gay Pride
parades anymore; in 1992, a gay and lesbian band played in
the Clinton inaugural parade.

If you've got a set of pipes longing to be put to good use, call or write the Gay and Lesbian Association of Choruses, 1617 E. 22nd Avenue, Denver, Colorado 80205 (303-832-1526). Or, if your aptitude with instruments goes beyond playing the 'flute, you might want to write: Lesbian and Gay Bands of America, P.O. Box 57099, Washington, D.C. 20037.

GAY GODDESSES AND WHY WE LOVE THEM

Women. Gay men don't want to live with 'em, but gay culture wouldn't be the same without 'em. In fact, gay men adore (and in many cases have made rich) certain female icons. Contrary to popular belief, it's not that we want to *be* them, it's just that they're able to touch us in ways that straight men can't begin to imagine. Who are these sirens of the gay psyche?

Joan Crawford—Joan literally clawed her way from rags to riches. In her movies as well as real life, she was a survivor if there ever was one. It's no wonder that gay men respect her refusal to be held down.

Bette Davis—Alluring as hell but tough as nails, Bette spawned a whole species of gay men willing to call a spade a spade and smile while doing it. You know the type.

Judy Garland—Her voice revealed a tragic openness, a vulnerability she was fighting to overcome. Gay men connected with it. When she died, so did their fear of standing up to the hatred that drove them into their closets.

Madonna—Combining sex appeal with blond ambition (not to mention the beefcake in her videos), she struck a chord with gay men in the '80s as they strove to be better, stronger, and faster than straight men ever believed possible.

Bette Midler—Bette's unabridged ribald humor set a new standard for gay men inclined to take themselves too seriously. We were there for her and she for us at a time when she was a nobody and it wasn't chic to be gay. She hasn't forgotten and neither have we.

Diana Ross—She may have "started out in a one-room, rundown tenement slum," but her Supreme rise to the top proved to all of us that we can make it. In her sequined gowns and ermine, she shows us that the best revenge is living well. Call her *Miss* Ross.

Barbra Streisand—Whether it's her voice or her constant battle for absolute perfection, Barbra hits home with many of us. We can even forgive her for running braless through a field in a bad cowlneck sweater as long as she keeps pulling at our heartstrings with her music.

Mae West—Some still think she was a man in drag, and for good reason. Mae wasn't afraid to say what gay men (and many women) of the time only thought: "Is that a pistol in your pocket, or are you just glad to see me?" She inspired Madonna and continues to enthrall many gay men.

Tammy Wynette—Any woman who could be married five times and still write "Stand by Your Man" deserves recognition. With a heart of gold and nerves of steel, she even got Hillary to apologize for saying she was "no Tammy Wynette." How could she be? There's only one.

THE FAG HAG—
THE GAY MAN'S GIRL FRIDAY

The fag hag (a misnomer if there ever was one) gets a bad rap. Actually, she's a staple of gay culture. Not the unattractive woman who can't get a man, as often portrayed, the fag hag is a woman who finds gay men more interesting, funnier, and more enjoyable to be around than many of their straight counterparts. Who can blame her? Stylish and more worldly than most women (think of what she's seen hanging around all those gay men), the fag hag is the gay goddess on a more local, tangible level. She loves gay men and the feeling is mutual . . . usually.

MISTAKEN IDENTITY:
THE ROLE OF DRAG QUEENS

"Sex is like bridge: If you don't have a good partner,
you better have a good hand."
—CHARLES PIERCE, FEMALE IMPERSONATOR

Drag queens take the best of those glamorous gay goddesses and exaggerate it. Consider Charles Pierce, who hit the stage in the '60s playing everyone from Tallulah Bankhead to Eleanor Roosevelt. He was such a hit that one critic wrote, "He might give transvestism a good name, and have perfectly normal sailors rifling through their mothers' closets." Perfectly normal sailors? And Divine. Any man that made his film debut playing a former First Lady deserves more than a little respect.

Whether they do it for a living or only on Halloween, certain gay men have a penchant for donning women's clothing, and often look pretty good in it. But not *only* gay men enjoy slipping into something a little more comfortable now and then. Cross-dressing apparently is a favorite pastime of more than a few straight guys. The only difference: Gay men have the guts to do it in public.

Still, when it comes to drag, all men are *not* created equal. Some guys-as-gals can tantalize even the most hetero man, while others, despite best efforts and piles of money for costumes and Max Factor, end up looking like a botched hormone experiment. Short of surgery, not much can be done if nature did you wrong. For those with at least some prospect of pulling it off, expert assistance is available: Miss Vera's Finishing School for Boys Who Want to Be Girls, the academy for those who "dare to begin this exciting journey of femme-self discovery." (Miss Vera takes this very seriously.) With courses like Ballet I and Tu-Tu ("keeping you on your toes when you're in your heels") and Cinch Course ("wasp-waist corset training") taught by Miss Vera herself and Betty Beautiful, even the most masculine among us can discover his feminine side. If you think you're man enough to try womanhood, and want more information about Miss Vera's, write: P.O. Box 1331, Old Chelsea Station, New York, NY 10011.

A bit of advice: Budding drag queens should pull out all the stops in choosing a drag name. Names such as Binetha Sheets, Helen Bed, Marsha Dymes, and Sofonda Peters let the world know you're a good-time gal. But you'd better not become too enamored with your alter ego, especially if you happen to be a truck driver who sometimes goes by the name Pussy Galore. Few things are more embarrassing than turning and waving enthusiastically when you hear someone call out "Stella," only to find out that the gentleman was *not* referring to you.

"How many Zsa Zsa Gabors can there be in a room at one time?"

—RICHARD EASLEY, IN *OUTRAGEOUS!*

BEAUTY IS IN THE EYE OF THE BEHOLDER

Maybe you're a little reluctant to strap on a corset, or perhaps you're afraid your chest hair will ruin the look. Fear not. You too can do drag. Whether in leather, a uniform from your favorite armed service, or policeman's gear, dressing up is what you make of it and who you make of yourself. As Paul Lynde once said when asked why bikers wear leather, "Chiffon wrinkles so easily." You can even enter a beauty pageant—Mr. International Leather, perhaps?—without having to pour yourself into an evening gown or twirl fire batons. To all those men out there fantasizing about becoming a member of the Village People: Go ahead—make our day.

I LOVE THE NIGHTLIFE: GOING OUT GUIDE TO MAJOR CITIES

You can't sit home every night. Get out and have some fun.

Here's where:

☞

CITY	MONDAY	TUESDAY	WEDNESDAY
ATLANTA	**Velvet**—Park Pl. Monday is the only all-gay night at this hip dance club; other nights are mixed.	**The Armory**—Juniper, NE. Something for everyone: videos, shows, dancing, and three bars.	**Heretic**—Cheshire Bridge Rd. Leather/Western garb. Dancing and volleyball.
AUSTIN	**Manuel's**—Congress. Creative Mexican cuisine with gay clientele.	**Chain Drive**—Willow St. Levi's and leather, poseurs. **The Crossing**—Red River St. Big cruise bar.	**Charlie's**—Lavaca. Dance club good almost any weeknight. Sometimes sleazy. Young crowd.
BALTIMORE	**Central Station**—N. Charles. Restaurant and neighborhood bar. Good happy hour.	**The Custom House Saloon**—Custom House Ave. Something for everyone.	**Stagecoach**—Charles St. Country & Western dancing; rooftop café.
BOSTON	**The Metropolitan Health Club**—Columbus. Sweat off those weekend sins at this cruisy gym with an attractive clientele.	**Luxor**—Church St. Video bar. Go early. JOX sports-bar downstairs.	**Boston Ramrod**—Boylston St. Levi's and leather.
CHICAGO	**Foxy's**—W. Belmont. Dancing and live entertainment. Also: **Little Jim's**—N. Halsted. Neighborhood bar.	**Charlie's**—N. Broadway. Country & Western; occasional dance lessons.	**Roscoe's**—N. Halsted. Cozy, warm atmosphere with nice crowd and patio.

The Metro—6th St. Videos.
Hoedowns—Cheshire Bridge Rd. Country & Western dancing.

Bulldogs—Peachtree St., NE. Videos and self-styled "#1 cruise bar of Hotlanta." Very manly.

Backstreet—Peachtree St., NE. Big private dance club, open 24 hours on weekends. Young.

Blake's—10th St. Drag queens sing gospel music for preppies during happy hour 4—7.

San Francisco's—San Jacinto. Country & Western dance bar.

Oilcan Harry's—W. 4th. Dance club with Guppies and college boys. Good happy hour.

The 404—Colorado. Big dance club for the young and the restless—open till 6 a.m.

East Side Cafe—Manor Rd. Gay-owned, great brunch, and an outdoor area.

The Baltimore Eagle—N. Charles. Levi's and leather.
The Unicorn—Boston. Neighborhoody.

Allegro—Cathedral St. Dance club. Careful: Sometimes has women's night.

The Hippo—W. Eager. Big dance club. Also has videos and karaoke.

Leon's—Park Ave. Popular neighborhood bar.

Chaps—Huntington Ave. Dancing, videos, cruising; good most nights.

Quest—Boylston. Three floors of wildness. Dancing, with a patio on the roof. Or: **Napoleon Club**—Piedmont. Piano bar.

Club Café—Columbus Ave. at Berkeley. Restaurant, videos, live entertainment.
The Loft—Stanhope, behind Club Café. After-hours club.

On the Park—Shawmut & Union Park. Good brunch. Later: **Avalon**—Lansdowne St. Good dance spot; Sundays only.

Sidetrack—N. Halstead. Gay MTV: Videos with some theme nights.
Berlin—W. Belmont. Alternative videos, cruise bar.

Gentry—N. Rush. Happy hour. Later: **Manhole**—N. Halsted. Dance club. Leather, too.

Vortex—N. Halsted. Hot dance club with occasional shows.
Big Chicks—N. Sheridan. Dancing, pool, patio.

Crowbar—N. Kingsbury. New York-type dance bar. Dark and loud.

CITY	MONDAY	TUESDAY	WEDNESDAY
CLEVELAND	**Over the Rainbow**—Detroit. Neighborhoody bar, young crowd. Monday is best night.	**Leather Stallion Saloon**—St. Clair. You guessed it. Country & Western music with a patio area. Has early tea dance Sundays.	**Numbers Niteclub**—Frankfort. Video and dance bar. Good Wednesdays, but also Saturday and Sunday. Go late.
DENVER	**Garbo's**—E. 9th. Piano bar, jazz. Also check out: **Metro Express**—E. 13th Ave.	**Charlies**—E. Colfax. Country & Western dancing, very popular.	**The Den**—W. Colfax. You can eat there, then hang out until you meet someone.
HOUSTON	**Brazos River Bottom**—Brazos. Aka the "BRB." Popular Country & Western bar.	**The Ripcord**—Fairview. Leather bar. Also: **Montrose Mining Co.**—Pacific. Leather, cruisy.	**Gentry**—Richmond. Amateur strip contests are worth a look. Also: **Berry Hill**—Kuykendahl. Neighborhood bar, entertainment.
LOS ANGELES	**Cobalt Cantina**—Sunset. Delicioso Southwestern food in a casual atmosphere filled with interesting men. Or: **Marix**—N. Flores. Tex-Mex at its best, but always a wait.	**Mark's**—La Cienega. Northern Italian food; jammed with men. Covered sidewalk seating. Also: **The Abbey**—N. Robertson. Artsy coffee house with patio.	**Chit-Chat**—Third. Dial L for love in this hip diner filled with L.A.'s beautiful boys. Also: **Rage**—Santa Monica. Hot, loud dance club. Very fun.

THURSDAY	FRIDAY	SATURDAY	SUNDAY
Keys—W. 6th. Neighborhoody, with a cute crowd on Thursdays.	**The Artful Dodger**—W. 76th. For an intimate dinner; then: **Memoirs**—Detroit. For a nightcap.	**U4ia Niteclub**—Berea. Largest, hippest dance club in town.	**Ohio City Oasis**—W. 29th. Levi's and leather, Country & Western dancing.
Surf City Bar & Grill—E. Colfax. Popular restaurant with young crowd. Strippers.	**B.J.'s Carousel**—S. Broadway. Shows, volleyball, billiards, food, happy hour.	**Paradise Garage**—Fox St. Hot dance spot with young crowd.	**Footloose Café**—S. Broadway. Unwind with good food in a very gay atmosphere.
Rich's—San Jacinto. Disco that attracts big, fun young crowds. Also: **E.J.'s**—Ralph. Neighborhood bar with entertainment.	**Pacific Street**—Pacific. Good dance club, go-go boys. Also: **JR's**—Pacific. Food, videos. And: **Mary's**—Westheimer. Leather, patio.	**Heaven**—Hyde Park. Fun dance club. Also: **Inergy**—Hillcroft. Dancing, live entertainment.	**House of Pies**—Kirby. "House of Guys," a good place for breakfast or to pick up a slice on the way home. Tonight: **JR's**.
The Spike—Santa Monica. Levi's/leather cruise bar. Also: **Maxx**—Yucca. Alternative dance club. Very hot scene in very scary area.	**Revolver**—Santa Monica. Video bar with homogenous frat boy-like crowd. Also: **Temple**—Wilshire. Alternative dance club, young crowd.	**Arena**—Santa Monica. Large dance club, good mix. Also: **Asylum**—Santa Monica. Body boys and go-go dancers. Later: **The Probe**—N. Highland. After-hours dance party.	**Butterfield's**—Sunset. Start here with brunch. Then: **Mother Lode**—Santa Monica. Great afternoon beer bust. **Revolver**—Santa Monica. Videos.

CITY	MONDAY	TUESDAY	WEDNESDAY
MEMPHIS	**Amnesia**—Poplar. Restaurant, patio, videos, and dancing.	**Chaps**—N. Claybrook. Levi's and leather, two bars and a patio.	**The Apartment**—Madison. Multi-ethnic crowd. Also: **The Hut**—N. Cleveland. Neighborhood bar.
MIAMI	**Barrio**—Washington. Mexican dining and drag waiters. Or: **Century**—Ocean Dr. Attitude as Art. Then: **Less Bains**—Washington. Boys' Night.	**The Lazy Lizard**—Lincoln. Great Southwestern food and margaritas. Then: **Rebar**—Washington. Big Tuesday. Go-go boys.	**Club Body Tech**—Washington. Workout with Madonna. Then: **West End**—Lincoln Rd. Neighborhood bar with 3-4-1 happy hour, shows.

Pipeline—Poplar. Leather and Levi's, with a courtyard.

Reflections—N. Avalon. Two-stepping, entertainment.

J-Wags—Madison Ave. 24-hour dance club. Also: **Oops**—Autumn. As in "Oops, where did the time go?" Open 24 hours.

Rendezvous—Gen. Washburn Alley. Authentic barbecue. Mixed crowd.

Bang—Washington. See and be seen, and nibble on dinner. Then: **Twist**—Washington. Hot bi-level cruise bar. Later: **Kremlin**—Lincoln. Dance in a communist style.

Warsaw—Collins. Formerly No. 1 in Miami. When you're No. 2, you try harder. Suzanne Bartsch and New York drag shows.

Paragon—Collins. Before recent move, one of the world's hottest clubs. Still?

Tea Dance—various outdoor locations, 4–10 pm. Huge crowds al fresco, tunes, and drinks. **Amnesia**—3d & Collins. The world-famous Ibiza tea dance winters here until early summer, when it heads home to the Mediterranean. Also: **Warsaw** or **Twist.**

CITY	MONDAY	TUESDAY	WEDNESDAY
MINNEAPOLIS	**House of Breakfast—** Chicago. For a good breakfast to start the week off right. Tonight, dine at **24th on the Avenue—** Hennepin.	**Body Quest—N.** Aldrich. To burn off all those calories from yesterday. The scenery's not bad, either.	**Cafe Wyrd—W.** Lake. Get over the hump with a cup of coffee at this happening coffee house.
NEW ORLEANS	**Clover Grill—** Bourbon St. 24-hour Art Deco diner that packs the boys in. Or: **Petunia's—St.** Louis. Popular Cajun and Creole restaurant.	**Good Friends—** Dauphine. Cozy bar, open 24 hours. Mature crowd.	**The Phoenix—** Elysian Fields. 24-hour neighborhood leather and cruise bar; upstairs is **The Men's Room.**
NEW YORK	**Klosett Klub—W.** 14th St. Industrial music, erotic dancers, cabaret. **CB's Gallery—** Bowery (Bleecker). House music for East Village kids.	**Roxy—**18th St. & 10th. Gay roller skating. 1st Tue. is Calvin Klein undies; 2d Tue. is Speedos. **"Swirl" at Crowbar—**E. 10th St. Drag lessons by Girlina.	**"Lick It" at Limelight—**6th Ave. at 20th St. Two dance floors, go-go boys, and more. **Amadeus/DMSR—** Hudson St. Dancing, cruising in boxer shorts. **Cactus Club—** roving Country & Western rave.

Brass Rail—
Hennepin Ave.
Neighborhood bar
with 2-4-1 drinks.
Also:
Club Chaos—
Hennepin. Mixed
alternative dance
club.

The Saloon—
Hennepin. Hip
dance club, young
crowd. Also:
Club Metro—
Pierce Butler (St.
Paul). Dancing
and entertainment

Gay 90's—
Hennepin. One of
the hottest clubs
in the country,
with several bars,
game rooms, and
dinner. Also:
Rumours—Robert
St. (St. Paul). Popular
dance club.

Town House—
University Ave.
(St. Paul). Two-
stepping. **The
Rogue—**S. 5th St.
Restaurant.

Jewels Tavern—
Decatur.
Neighborhood
leather bar.

**Café Lafitte-in-
Exile—**Bourbon
St. The country's
oldest continuously
open gay bar. A
must. Also:
Corner Pocket—
St. Louis. Live
entertainment.

Parade Disco—
Bourbon St. Hot
men and music,
and a great
balcony. Also:
Rawhide—
Burgundy. Leather
and Country &
Western.

The Mint—
Esplanade Ave.
Afternoon cabaret
is jammed. Then:
**The Bourbon
Pub—**Bourbon St.
Tea dance.

The Break—8th
Ave. at 22d St. This
neighborhood bar
features 2-4-1
Margaritas. **The
Townhouse—**E.
58th at 3d. Drinks
or dinner; professional
crowd.
Champs—W. 19th
St. Sports bar; "Cheers"
for queers.

Splash—W. 17th St.
Wet amd wild, especially
for happy hour. <u>Do</u> drop
the soap.
**Sound Factory
Bar—**W. 21st St.
High energy dance
club. **The Spike—**
11th Ave. at 20th.
NYC's preeminent
leather bar.
Inconsistent crowd
quality. Late:
Zone DK—W.
21st at West Side
Hwy. Anything
goes.

Roxy—18th St. &
10th. The hottest
disco. **"Spunk"
at Crowbar—**E.
10th St. Good
crowd, music, and
back room. **Sound
Factory—**W. 27th
St. (not the Fri.
place)—After-
hours, no drinks.
Hot tunes.

The Works—
Columbus Ave.
Popular Beer
Blast attracts
crowds of preps.
U.S.A.—47th St.
at Broadway.
Hot go-go boys.
**Uncle
Charlie's—**
Greenwich Ave.
Landmark video
bar. Drink
specials.

| --- | --- | --- | --- |
PHILADELPHIA	**12th Street GYM—** If Rocky were gay he'd work out here.	**Woody's**—13th between Walnut and Locust. Two-level bar and dance club with two-stepping Tuesdays.	**Millenium Coffee Shop—** S. 12th. Hip crowd. Then: **2-4 Club**—St. James St. Dance club, open late.
ST. LOUIS	**Blanche's**—N. Sarah. Family-owned with a nice patio. Eclectic crowd.	**Angles**—Choutreau. Something for everyone: dancing, drag, leather, and food.	**Clemen-tine's—** Menard. Leather and Levi's, with a patio. Also: **Alley Bar & Grill—** 17th St. Dancing, food, multi-ethnic.
SAN FRANCISCO	**Stud**—9th & Harrison. Funk night. Also pinball and pool. A fave. Or: **Midnight Sun—** 18th St. Happy hour specials. **Metro**—16th St. Chinese food, cool young crowd.	**Detour**—Market & Castro. Beer bust. **The Mint—** Market. Food and videos.	**Tilt**—Howard. Hip mixed crowd, imported DJs. Or: **Rawhide II—** 7th St. Country & Western two-stepping lessons. Also: **Elephant Walk—** 18th & Castro. Piano bar.

THURSDAY	FRIDAY	SATURDAY	SUNDAY
Judy's—3d & Banbridge. Creative American cuisine, cool crowd. Then: **Raffles**—S. Camac. Country & Western and piano bar.	**Woody's**—Good happy hour. Then: **Rodz**—Rodman. For dinner on the rooftop patio or show tunes in the piano bar.	**Bike Stop**—S. Quince. Leather bar downstairs, sports bar upstairs. Then: Dance at **Woody's**. Later: **2-4 Club** for after-hours action.	**Circa**—Walnut. Popular eats. Then: **Club Revival**—S. 3d St. Alternative dance club with young crowd.
Fallout—Washington. Alternative dance club for young hipsters.	**The Loading Zone**—S. Euclid. Videos, good happy hour. Also: **Redel's**—Debaliviere. Popular restaurant.	**Magnolia's**—S. Vandeventer. Five bars, dancing. Restaurant, too.	**Café Balaban's**—N. Euclid. For dinner. Then: **Gabriel's Club**—S. Broadway. Neighborhood bar for a nightcap.
Trocadero—4th St. Dance all night. Also: **Box**—Divisadero. Great dance mixes. Staying power. Or: **Josie's Cabaret & Juice Joint**—16th St. Comedy, cabaret. **Star 69**—Natoma. Club kids partying late.	**Mad Madelaine's Mad House at End Up**—6th at Harrison. Erotic and neurotic. Or: **The Headquarters**—Castro. Uniforms, leather. Then: **Love Factory**—Harrison. After-hours action.	**Lone Star**—Harrison. Biker beer bust 3–7. Then: **Spread**—Folsom at 6th. Three dance floors, wild action, young crowd. **Club Universe**—Townsend. Dance club with changing themes.	**Pleasure-dome**—Townsend at 3d. Largest gay dance club. Beautiful boys and club kids. Or: **Eagle**—11th & Harrison. Beer bust, best 4–6 pm. **Badlands**—18th St. Beer bust 4–on.

CITY	MONDAY	TUESDAY	WEDNESDAY
SEATTLE	**Brass Connection**— E. Pike. Dinner, entertainment, young crowd.	**The Madison Bar & Grill**—E. Madison. Videos. Or: **Hombres**— 14th Ave. Levi's and leather, neighborhood bar.	**Timberline Tavern**—Boren Ave. Lodge-like setting with Country & Western dancing.
WASHINGTON	**Annie's Paramount Steak House**—17th St., NW. Great beef dishes; jammed with men, mostly older. An institution.	**La Cage Aux Follies**—S. Capitol St., SE. Exotic dancers. Known as "dollar d—k night" or the "petting zoo." Or: **Bachelor's Mill**— 8th St., SE. Mostly African-American men.	**The Green Lantern**—L St., NW. Aka "The Green Latrine." Cruising as an art form. **The D.C. Eagle**—New York Ave., NW. Levi's and leather. Or: **El Faro**—18th St., Dancing, shows. NW. Food, mostly Latino crowd.

THURSDAY	FRIDAY	SATURDAY	SUNDAY
Re-Bar—Howell. Contempo mixed dance club, but Thursday is gay night.	**Double Header**— 2d Ave. Neighborhood bar; one of U.S.'s oldest.	**Thumpers**—E. Madison. Food, videos, patio. Or: **Neighbours**— Broadway. Hot dance club. Been around for years.	**Hamburger Mary's**— Broadway E. Burgers and dancing. Eclectic.
Trumpet's—17th St., NW. Good food and packed for drinks after. Also: **Remington's**— Pennsylvania Ave., SE. Country & Western dancing. Friendly crowd.	**JR's**—17th St., NW. Jammed happy hour. Later: **Badlands**—22d St., NW. Dark and smoky, but hot guys and good music (usually). Then: **Frat House**— P St., NW. Late-night action, movies.	**Tracks**—K St., SE. D.C.'s biggest, wildest club with dancing till dawn. Club kids galore. Or: **The Fireplace**— P St., N.W. Cruise bar with neighborhoody feeling. Also: **Ziegfeld's**—1/2 St., SE. Popular drag shows.	**Perry's**— Columbia Rd., NW. Drag brunch. Great show, good food, and pretty crowd. **JR's**— 17th St., N.W. Afternoon drink specials. Then: **Herb's**— 17th St., N.W. Burgers and boys.

A MAN FOR ALL SEASONS:
RATING THE BIG ANNUAL EVENTS

Gay men have elevated life, liberty, and the pursuit of happiness (particularly the latter) to new heights. Those with seemingly limitless time and money can spend the entire year jet-setting from venue to venue, doing the "circuit" of big annual events. The rest of us stay home wondering, "How *do* they do it?" For those who can do it all, here are some of the highlights of the annual social calendar:

January

Winterfest/Gay Ski Week—Park City/Deer Valley, Utah, second week of January. Actually, one of several gay ski weeks held every year, including those in Aspen during the third week of January, and Lake Tahoe in March, in addition to international ski resorts. Winterfest attracts some three thousand thrill-seekers. Ski by day, party by night, with the Snow Ball and Winter White Party. A drag ski event tops it off.

February

Blue Ball—Philadelphia, early February. This weekend of parties, the biggest of which is Saturday night's Blue Ball, is a relatively recent addition to the circuit, and one which is still working out the bugs. With the considerable hometown talent and the proximity of the huge gay populations of New York, Washington, and Baltimore, this event promises to get better and better with practice. Don't we all? The proceeds benefit AIDS Information Network.

The Hearts Party—Valentine's Weekend, Chicago. This is Chicago's big blowout, featuring a Friday night party, Saturday night no-holds-barred partying in heart-themed garb, and Sunday activities for survivors. A great way to take off the chill.

The Winter Party—Valentine's Weekend, South Beach Miami. This noon-to-dusk party on the beach at 15th Street benefits Safeguarding American Values for Everyone. Although a newcomer to the circuit, the party draws rave reviews. It has been compared to the GMHC Morning Party on Fire Island.

The Saint-at-Large White Party—Presidents' Day Weekend, New York (often at Roseland). This all-night extravaganza (and its mate, the Black Party) are the gay granddaddies of the circuit. If you like wildlife, this event is for you. Check your clothes and your inhibitions at the door.

The Apollo Ball—First Saturday in February, Birmingham, Alabama. The Mystic Krewe of Apollo (with sister krewes in Tuscaloosa, Lafayette, Baton Rouge, and other Southern towns) throws this annual black-tie bash for its members and two thousand invited guests. A twenty-year-old gay social and charitable organization, Apollo gives "Southern hospitality" new meaning.

Mardi Gras—New Orleans, February or March. No one parties like the queens in this professional party town. The charm of the *Vieux Carré* and the mayhem of Mardi Gras are musts for anyone who really likes to have a good time. The best partying is on the weekend, Monday and (Fat) Tuesday immediately preceding Ash Wednesday.

March

The Saint-at-Large Black Party—St. Patrick's Day Weekend, New York (often Roseland). Just as you're coming down from the White Party, this more decadent party hits (so to speak). Caligula meets Nero in Sodom. Not for the faint-hearted.

Night of 1,000 Gowns—New York, third weekend of March. Drag at its best. The crowning of the Emperor and Empress of New York's Imperial Court. Proceeds benefit a number of charitable organizations.

April

The White Party in Palm Springs—Easter weekend in Palm Springs, California. The local Easter parade was nothing like this. Hot men in a hot desert bring welcome relief from winter's chill in a series of three parties. The big one is at the Convention Center. Party central (and the best boy watching) is at the Marquis Hotel. When it's all over, you'll feel as if *you* need to be resurrected.

Spring to Life—Late April or early May in Washington, D.C. This charitable weekend of events got its start during the 1993 March on Washington. Spring to Life's biggest event is the Saturday night blowout party, held at the historic Old Post Office. There's also a dinner (those Washington queens love fancy dinners), morning party, and barbecue. Although not yet a mainstay on the circuit, the cherry blossoms themselves are worth the trip.

Splash Day—Last Sunday in April, Austin, Texas. This day of wet fun, the culmination of a weekend of debauchery, is Texas's answer to Hotlanta. It's held at Hippy Hollow, a nude bathing lake. Attracts lots of brazen out-of-towners. If you miss the April event, they reprise it the Sunday before Labor Day. Don't forget the sunscreen.

May

Memorial Day in Pensacola—A BIG event, especially for Southern girls. Warm Gulf waters and *hot* bods—as many as thirty-five thousand of them. Five to six miles of beach filled with 100% gay American males. The only problem is inadequate nightlife. Organizers are starting to catch on, and have held a White Party. Most of the action is at huge block parties in the streets.

June

Gay Pride—New York and San Francisco (both on the last weekend). Of course plenty of other cities have Gay Pride Days, but New York and San Francisco are the biggest and therefore (as any size queen will tell you) the best. In New York, highlights are the parade down Fifth Avenue, the Pride Dance along the Hudson River in Greenwich Village, and the lavender lighting of the Empire State Building. Just being in San Francisco, the capital of the gay world, for Gay Freedom Day is exhilarating.

July

Provincetown Fourth of July—Provincetown, Massachusetts. A huge draw for guys from all over the country, but mostly east of the Mississippi, P'town offers small-town coziness combined with big-city partying.

Russian River Fourth of July—Outside San Francisco. The West Coast version of the P'town Fourth, attracting revelers from all over the country, but mostly west of the Continental Divide (that's a geographic marker, not a body part). Gambol in the woods; just watch out for poison ivy (that's a plant, not a drag queen).

August

Hotlanta—Atlanta, first weekend in August. Begun in 1979, this event calls itself the largest gay party in the world. Whether that's true or not, it *is* a sight for sore eyes. A whirlwind of official and unofficial parties, the Mr. Hotlanta contest, and the Sunday raft race on the Chattahoochee River combine to make this the Mother of All Hangovers.

Crepe Myrtle Festival—Mid-August in Chapel Hill, North Carolina. Get out your hoopskirts for this one. Started over a decade ago as a private party at No. 2 Maple Drive, this party has grown to be a regional phenomenon, attracting men from all over the Southeast to see the beautiful crepe myrtle and other flora. Proceeds benefit local AIDS charities.

GMHC Morning Party—Fire Island, third weekend of August. Started in 1983, and benefiting Gay Men's Health Crisis, this event has become a jewel in the circuit crown, attracting men from as far away as L.A. It's held during gay morning, i.e., afternoon, so if you go out the night before (and everyone does), it makes for a very long weekend. Get plenty of sleep in advance and take Monday off.

September

Labor Day L.A.—Los Angeles, Labor Day weekend. This four-day series of fundraisers for numerous AIDS organizations and other gay charities is one of the highlights of the year. The beautiful weather, friendly natives, and hordes of out-of-town visitors combine with an incredible roster of imaginative events only Tinsel Town could pull off to make this an absolute must on everyone's social calendar.

Wigstock—New York, Labor Day. This day-long drag event in Tompkins Square (the East Village) features high hair, beautiful boys, and all varieties of performers. Not a circuit party, but a blast if you're in the area.

The Red Party—Columbus, Ohio, last weekend in September. After fifteen years, the organizers have now made it the Red & Black Party. Who knows if the innovation will stick? Over two thousand men, including many out-of-towners, flock to Ohio's state capital (sometimes called the best gay town in the U.S.) for a blowout party.

Anatole Hotel Black Tie Dinner—Dallas, last weekend in September. This gay charity event is reportedly the largest sit-down dinner in Dallas, and is believed to be the largest black tie dinner in the country. Texans sure do things big.

October

Artrageous—Nashville, third weekend in October. Promenade from art gallery to art gallery for cocktail parties, art purchases, and mingling with Nashville's in-set. End up at the Vanderbilt Stadium Club for a big dance party and art auction. Proceeds benefit Nashville Cares, a local AIDS organization.

Halloween—New Orleans, Halloween weekend. Two nights and a day of parties benefiting local AIDS charities, this weekend attracts men from all over the country. The schedule includes a welcoming party at a fun location (the zoo, an

amusement park, etc.), a giant costume party, and a Sunday jazz brunch with delicious New Orleans food and the official New Orleans beverage—anything with alcohol in it. For outrageous costumes, this is second only to Mardi Gras.

—New York. Big annual bacchanals like Suzanne Bartsch's extravaganza, and streets teeming with costumed revelers throughout Greenwich Village and Chelsea. Anything goes.

—San Francisco. Of course, the gay national holiday is celebrated in the capital of the gay world. Much like Halloween in the Village, Halloween in the Castro is a spectacle to behold.

—Key West, Halloween weekend. This island getaway is always weird and wild but particularly during Halloween's "Fantasy Fest."

—Washington, D.C. Slightly tamer (only slightly) and smaller than New York's and San Francisco's celebrations, the annual "Great High Heel Race" and relatively new Halloween dance bring high camp to the nation's capital. Not yet on the circuit, but a lot of fun if you're in the 'hood.

November

Fundraisers—All month, most metropolitan areas. DIFFA (Design Industry Foundation for AIDS), AmFAR (American Foundation for AIDS Research), NGLTF (National Gay and

Lesbian Task Force), Human Rights Campaign Fund, and many, many more. Not circuit parties (and, unfortunately, sometimes not much fun), but *important* to do. Dust off your tux and shell out some bucks.

The White Party—Thanksgiving weekend, Miami. Referred to as *The* White Party, this annual bash at the onetime glamorous (but hurricane-battered) Vizcaya estate attracts four thousand revelers. The bodies are celestial, but three nights of partying before the big event often leave the attendees somewhat tired. Proceeds go to the Health Crisis Network.

GMHC Dance-A-Thon—New York, late November, early December. Held at the Jacob Javits Convention Center, this marathon has raised as much as $2 million in one weekend alone for Gay Men's Health Crisis. It attracts top entertainment and DJs.

December

New Year's Eve in Miami—What better place to ring out the old and ring in the new than this sunny, warm city basking in the limelight of its own rebirth? Gorgeous gays from all over the globe party at Paragon, Warsaw, and the other hot spots or merely soak up the sun and sights of South Beach. It sure beats freezing your butt off in Times Square just to watch some ball drop.

Gay Cruise Week

DO UNTO OTHERS ... SOME SUGGESTIONS FOR THOSE FLEETING MOMENTS WHEN YOU REMEMBER THAT THE WORLD DOES *NOT* REVOLVE AROUND YOU

"For Christ's sake, open your mouths; don't you people get tired of being stepped on?"

—BETTE MIDLER

We don't all lead lives of privileged leisure, with everything money can buy. (We don't all have beautiful tans either.) But one quality we all can be proud of is the generosity and commitment to others that gay men have demonstrated, particularly in recent years.

In the wake of the AIDS epidemic, gay men have responded to the call for help in ways that most fundraisers never thought possible. The gay community has become expert not only in raising the dough but raising the spirits of those in need through volunteerism. Whether it's lending a hand in the battle to combat AIDS or assisting some other worthy cause, gay men are blessed with the time, and often the resources, to make a real difference.

But those willing to offer their time and money often find themselves besieged by organizations representing every possible special interest, from the policemen's ball to Mothers Against Bedwetters. Where does one draw the line? Everyone should do *something* for someone other than himself (tipping bartenders doesn't count). If you can't afford to donate money, donate your time. Better yet, do both if you can. One night a week not spent in the bars won't kill you. For those who don't know where to begin, here are just a few of the many national groups worthy of your support:

American Foundation for AIDS Research (AmFAR)
1515 Broadway, Suite 3601
New York, New York 10036

National Association of People with AIDS
1413 K Street, N.W., No. 10
Washington, D.C. 20005

Gay & Lesbian Alliance Against Defamation
(GLAAD)
150 West 26th Street
New York, New York 10001

National Federation of Parents and Friends of
Lesbians and Gays (P-FLAG)
1012 14th Street, N.W., 7th Floor
Washington, D.C. 20005

LAMBDA Legal Defense Fund
666 Broadway, 12th Floor
New York, New York 10012

National Gay Youth Network
P.O. Box 846
San Francisco, California 94101

Names Project AIDS Memorial Quilt
1613 K Street, N.W.
Washington, D.C. 20006

Of course, these aren't the only groups worthy of your time and money. There are numerous worthwhile *local* organizations in every city and town that deserve your support as much or more than the larger national organizations. Organizations such as free clinics, hospices, AIDS buddy services, counseling services for gay youths, hotlines, and food banks all desperately depend on your contributions. If politics is your shtick, think about the Human Rights Campaign Fund, the AIDS Action Council, the Gay and Lesbian Victory Fund, and the National Gay and Lesbian Task Force. These groups fight to protect our rights to hold hands in public, live together, do drag, or whatever else being gay means to you. Support them.

ON THE ROAD TO RIO AND OTHER GREAT GAY GETAWAYS

"Not too much culture, please. I'm on my holiday."
—GEORGE DE LA PENA, *NIJINSKY*

Gay men are a restless group, not staying in one place very long before picking up, overstuffing their steamer trunks with outfits and toiletries, and hopping on a plane for some distant destination. While gay men are known to trot the entire globe, there are a number of stateside vacation spots that spring to mind when planning a gay getaway:

Where to go: **FIRE ISLAND, NEW YORK**

Why to go there: Because it's a legendary gay playground, having been popular for over forty years. Fab private parties and happy hunting grounds for those in search of . . .

Where to stay: Someone's **summer house** in the **Pines,** or, as a second choice, **Cherry Grove.** If you can't finagle an invitation, try the **Botel, Fire Island Pines** bed & breakfast, **Belvedere** guest house and cottages (Cherry Grove), or **Cherry Grove Beach Hotel** (part of which is the night spot the **Ice Palace**).

Where to eat:	Mostly **at home** or some fabu' **dinner party;** provisions can be purchased at the **Pines Pantry** ("$200 tomatoes"). For a dinner out, try the **Monster** (Cherry Grove).
Where to play:	**Blue Whale Bar** (the Pines)—credited with inventing tea dance in 1966; still has *the* tea dance on the Island. After midnight, at the **Pavillion** (the Pines), you can dance till dawn. Also, the **Ice Palace** (Cherry Grove) can be fun.
Miscellany:	No cars make this a great place. Know the daily ritual before arriving (timing is everything). Check out the condom trees in the Meatrack, also known as the Judy Garland Memorial Forest, between the Pines and Cherry Grove. If you can't remember his name, *Emily's Pines Phone Book* (called "The Queens Directory") lists F.I. residents by first name, and—if all you can remember is where he lives—by address.

Where to go:	**KEY WEST, FLORIDA**
Why to go there:	Because it's the most popular gay resort in the country and you can still get a tan in the winter (unlike Fire Island, P'town, or Rehoboth). It's an off-beat place with many gay-owned shops, galleries, and other establishments. What more do you want?
Where to stay:	*Not* at a big hotel. Try **Lighthouse Court,** an incredible complex of tropical gardens, sundecks, Jacuzzi and pool, or one of the wonderful guest houses, such as the **Marquesa Hotel** (mostly straight, but deluxe), **Alexander's, Big Ruby's Guesthouse,** the **Oasis,** or the **Brass Key Guesthouse.**
Where to eat:	**Mangoe's** (casual and reasonable), **Café**

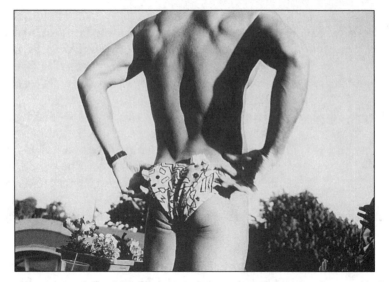

Marquesa (new American), **Antonia's** (Northern Italian), or **Croissants de France** (good for breakfast, inside or out).

Where to play: The **Copa—Key West** (for dancing), **801 Bar** or **Saloon 1** (for cruising), or **Key West Cabaret** (for live entertainment). On Sundays, go to **tea dance** outdoors at **La Terraza di Marti** ("La-Te-Da"), and later the **Atlantic Shores.**

Miscellany: Go to the **pier** at the end of the island at **sunset** to watch the sun go down and the wild **street performers** come out. "**Fantasy Fest**" is fun for **Halloween.**

Where to go: **PROVINCETOWN, MASSACHUSETTS**

Why to go there: Its natural beauty and teeming gay population *in season;* its tranquility and artists *off.*

Where to stay: One of the quaint guest houses, such as the **Anchor Inn,** the **Boatslip,** the **Brass Key Guesthouse,** the **Chicago House, Haven House,** or **Six Webster Place.** Or rent a

house for a week. Call a realtor well in advance. The **Business Guild** (gay businesses) number is 800-637-8696.

Where to eat: The **Boatslip, Franco's by the Sea, Mews, Pucci's Harborside,** and **Sal's Place.**

Where to play: **Herring Cove Beach** (gay beach), **Long Nook Beach** (in Truro) (nude bathing), **poolside** at the **Boatslip;** later, tea dance at the **Boatslip,** post-tea dance at the **Pied Piper** (men have to exit before sunset), and after-dinner dancing at the **Atlantic House Hotel** (the "**A-House**"), the **Love Shack, Rooster Bar,** or **Back Street.** End the evening at **Spiritus** for pizza and last-minute husband-hunting.

Miscellany: Only a gay resort would nickname the front of City Hall the "**Meatrack.**" **Fourth of July** and August's **Carnival Week** are big here. You can do the whole in-town tacky tourist shtick or you can escape and discover P'town's natural beauty. **Whale watch** or get a permit and build a fire on the beach at dusk with your main squeeze. Great arts community, too.

Where to go: **PALM SPRINGS, CALIFORNIA**

Why to go there: Because it's hot and dry in the winter, and if you like to golf or play tennis, it's paradise. Palm Springs is part faded Hollywood glitz, part L.A. excess, part pure tack, something like the Siegfried & Roy of resorts.

Where to stay: The **Marquis** (homo central for the **White Party**), the **Ritz-Carlton** (one of the most beautiful in the country), **Two Bunch Palms** (exclusive spa getaway for Hollywood's reclusive glitterati), and the **Abbey West** (deluxe accommodations with on-premises gym), **Harlow Club Hotel** and **Hacienda en Sueño** (both luxurious).

Where to eat: Who eats? People go to P.S. to show off their girlish figures, not to pig out. Still, you might try the **Café** at the **Desert Palms, Shame on the Moon,** gay-owned **Crayons Cafe** (Cathedral City), or **Bangkok Five** (Rancho Mirage).

Where to play: The **Desert Palms Hotel pool** for sunbathing *and* cruising, **C.C. Construc-**

tion Co. (Country & Western *and* dance music, Levi's and leather, young crowd), and **Daddy's** (**Daddy Warbuck's**) (whipped cream wrestling—no lie). The **private parties** are some of the best nightlife.

Miscellany: "P.S. I Love You," as *tout le monde* calls it, is really a string of five towns, **P.S., Cathedral City** (ironically most of the gay bars are here), **Rancho Mirage, Palm Desert,** and **Indian Wells.** Best time for partying is **Easter** for the **White Party.** Check out *The Bottom Line,* P.S.'s gay weekly for info on the scene. Go somewhere else in the summer; the heat will kill you (or at least do a number on your 'do).

Where to go: **REHOBOTH BEACH, DELAWARE**

Why to go there: Because it's a quaint town with a growing gay presence. And besides, it's the only gay resort worth visiting between Fire Island and South Beach.

203

Where to stay:	Try the **Silver Lake Guest House** for commodious, gay-owned accommodations in a pleasant setting on a lake and a block from Poodle Beach. The new **Mallard Guest House** is also nice. The **Sandcastle** and **Brighton Suites** are well located, but with a very mixed clientele.
Where to eat:	Have breakfast at the **Royal Treat** (tell Doris you want a table on the porch), or pick up some pastries on the way to the beach at **Cosmic Bakery.** Skip lunch or grab something on the boardwalk. Dine in high (but casual) style at any one of a number of gay-friendly restaurants, including the **Blue Moon, La La Land,** the **Celsius,** or **Square One. Adriatico** has great basic Italian food. For the ultimate in casual dining *al fresco,* try **Chicken Ed's.**
Where to play:	Two gay beaches: **Poodle Beach** (aka "**Poodle Point**"), at the south end of town, and **North Shores** in **Henlopen State Park.** *The* place for happy hour is the **Blue Moon,** whose proprietress, **Joyce Felton,** is a longtime friend of, and fighter for, the gay community. A cozy place for after-dinner drinks is **La La Land**'s patio. Later, dance till you drop at the urbane but on-again, off-again **Strand,** or the more rustic mainstay, the **Renegade.**
Miscellany:	The occasional tension between the gay community and some of the locals (the "Keep-Rehoboth-a-family-town" crowd) and a few redneck visitors keeps it interesting. Just avoid the boardwalk games and tacky T-shirt shops. One of the best aspects of Rehoboth is its **summer residents,** drawn from Philadelphia, Baltimore, and Washington, making for a pretty diverse and just plain *pretty* crowd.

Where to go: **RUSSIAN RIVER, CALIFORNIA**

Why to go there: If you're the woodsy type that likes **hiking, camping, horseback riding,** and **nature walks** among the **redwoods,** this place is for you. And if the beach and the beef parade aren't your scene, you might prefer Russian River to one of the ocean resorts.

Where to stay: **Fife's Resort** (quiet and well-appointed cabins), the **Woods Resort** (set back in the), **Highlands Resort** (cozy cabins), the **Willows Guest House** (on the river), or the **Highland Dell Inn** (restored Victorian B&B on the river).

Where to eat: **River Inn Restaurant** (home cookin'), **Breeze-Inn Bar-B-Q** (takeout and delivery), **Burdon's** (romantic ambience), or **Little Bavaria** (year-round Oktoberfest-like atmosphere).

Where to play: Swim in the river near **Wohler Bridge** or at one of the resorts; after dinner, start at **Fife's** (piano bar), barhop to **Molly Brown's Saloon** for Country & Western music, then on to **Rainbow Cattle Company** (a

Miscellany:

neighborhoody bar), and end up at **Ziggurat** (dance club in a converted theater). The center of the gay action is **Guerneville,** but neighboring towns (**Forestville, Monte Rio,** and **Rio Nido**) are nice, too. **Napa** and **Sonoma** wineries are twenty to sixty minutes away, and **Calistoga,** with **hot springs** and **mud baths** (à la Montecatini), is an hour away.

Where to go: **SAUGATUCK, MICHIGAN**

Why to go there: If you live in the Midwest, this is your best (and closest) bet. It's got the woodsy charm of Russian River and the Esther Williams water sports of Key West, without the occasional attitude of Fire Island or South Beach, all within a few hours of both Detroit and Chicago.

Where to stay: **Douglas Dunes Resort** (the center of the nighttime action), **Academy Place** (pool), the **Kirby House** B&B (charming), **Moore's Creek Inn** (1873 farmhouse), or **Camp It** (for those who like roughing it).

Where to eat: **Kalico Kitchen** (breakfast or after-the-bar pig-out); **Café Sir Douglas**, or **What Knot.**

Where to play: Catch rays on **Oval Beach** (where the boys are), the **private beach** (some nude sunbathing), or on one of the boats anchored off the beach. After a shower, stop by **tea dance** at **Douglas Dunes;** then, after dinner, back to the **Dunes.** If you haven't met someone by the end of the evening, satisfy another urge at the **Kalico Kitchen.**

Miscellany: Good **antique shops** are all over this area; bring plastic. Get to know some of the regulars who have or rent homes in Saugatuck or in one of the nearby towns, **Douglas, South Haven,** and **Holland.** The latter has a *stunning* tulip festival in the spring.

Where to go: **SOUTH BEACH, MIAMI**

Why to go there: Because it is *the* hottest, coolest, hippest gay mecca—at least for now—and the international center for fashion photography. The weather is great year-round (although June–September can get a little sticky), and the nightlife is *fab.*

Where to stay: **The Raleigh** (Art Deco palace with pool memorialized in Kelly Klein's book), **Marlin Hotel** (a blend of Deco/Caribbean, and a reputed haunt of Madonna), **Hotel Impala** (known for its service), and the **Century** (a fave of fashion photographers). Or, if you want a place to escape the action, call the **Bed & Breakfast Service** for a recommendation; ask for a cottage on a **Coconut Grove** estate.

Where to eat: With few exceptions, the food in Miami is not the main attraction. After looking at all those trim bronzed bods, you may opt for

Slimfast and celery sticks. If you want to throw caution to the winds, try the **Century** (ultra-trendy food and PiBs, but don't cut yourself on the metal menus), **A Fish Called Avalon** (very popular), the **Strand** (see and be seen), **Pacific Time** (good Pacific Rim cuisine), and the **Palace** (your food will get cold while your head swivels, checking out the action).

Where to play: See *"I Love the Nightlife,"* above. Spend the day on the **beach** between **12th and 22nd. Paragon** on Saturday night and Sunday afternoon's roving **outdoor tea dance** or **Amnesia** are musts.

Miscellany: For a real taste of South Beach, try to meet some of the locals. **Louis Canales,** the "Mayor of South Beach," and **Kitty Meow** (you don't have to ask, do you?) are two prominent figures. Stay out of seedy areas, such as around the airport, and try not to look like a tourist if you find yourself there. Bring or rent rollerblades to look like a real regular.

TAKING A GROUP SUMMER HOUSE

"I wonder if Socrates and Plato took a house on Crete during the summer."
—**WOODY ALLEN, IN** *LOVE AND DEATH*

The popularity among gay men of such summer resort spots as Rehoboth, Ogunquit, and Saugatuck has put these towns on the map—much to the chagrin of some of their year-round residents. Each Friday night from Memorial to Labor Day, jeeps, BMWs, and Saab convertibles filled with attractive men anxious to work on their tans line the highways. Sunday afternoon sees the same guys, often a little worse for wear, heading back to reality while rehashing who slept with whom and complaining about some waiter with attitude and a fake British accent at the latest chichi resort restaurant.

Regrettably, resort living isn't cheap. This means that summering at the beach, the country, or the mountains often involves splitting the cost of a place with a group of friends (and sometimes strangers). If you didn't know them well before, you will by fall.

Sharing a summer house with a group of gay men fosters a sense of family. You eat together, sleep together, primp together, and talk about the rest of the town behind their backs together. What could be more fun? Something about seeing your friends roll out of bed the morning after a night of dancing on the speakers in their underwear binds you inextricably together. Some group houses adopt clever names and logos, and even have T-shirts printed. Other houses don't need logos; they have reputations. By Labor Day, if the people in your house are still speaking, they will have found the true meaning of friendship—until they dump you for somebody cuter next season.

THE ROCK OF AGES: TWENTY-FIVE YEARS OF GAY LIBERATION

The year 1969 isn't just a milestone in the gay movement; it's our Plymouth Rock. We've come a long way since the *San Francisco Examiner* described gay men as "semi-males" and "drag darlings." The ongoing battle for equal rights has become a part of the very fabric of gay culture. No exposé on gay life would be complete without homage to the people and events that have shaped our collective consciousness over the last twenty-five years. A few of the many individuals and events that have helped to make Gay Pride a reality, not just a parade, are remembered below:

June 27, 1969—The patron saint of gay men, Judy Garland, is buried in Westchester, New York. After midnight that night, police raid the Stonewall Inn in Greenwich Village and spark two consecutive nights of rioting.

October 20, 1969—The National Institute of Mental Health recommends that the United States repeal laws making homosexual sex between consenting adults illegal.

April 7, 1970—The Best Picture Oscar goes to *Midnight Cowboy,* the first movie containing sex between two men to win the award.

June 25, 1972—William Johnson, the first openly gay minister of the United Church of Christ, is ordained.

October 15, 1973—Dr. Harold Brown, a former New York City Health Commissioner, announces the formation of the National Gay Task Force (predecessor of NGLTF).

July 3, 1975—The U.S. Civil Service Commission repeals its ban on the employment of gay men and women.

September 8, 1975—Air Force Sergeant Leonard Matlovich appears on the cover of *Time* with the headline "I Am a Homosexual."

February 10, 1976—Andy Lippincott, a character in Gary Trudeau's *Doonesbury*, comes out. Five out of 450 papers that carry the comic strip refuse to print the series addressing Lippincott's sexuality.

November 8, 1977—Harvey Milk becomes the first openly gay man elected to the San Francisco Board of Supervisors. Also elected, former policeman Dan White.

November 7, 1978—California voters overwhelmingly reject Proposition 6—the Briggs Initiative—which would have banned gay people from teaching in public schools.

November 27, 1978—Having recently resigned his seat, disgruntled San Francisco Supervisor Dan White assassinates Mayor George Moscone and Supervisor Harvey Milk in City Hall. White is later sentenced to less than eight years.

October 14, 1979—Over 100,000 people participate in the first National March on Washington for Gay and Lesbian Rights.

May 30, 1980—High school senior Aaron Fricke takes his boyfriend to the prom after seeking a court order to be able to do so.

January 20, 1981—Ronald Reagan is inaugurated as the 40th President of the United States. Take two giant steps back.

August 2, 1981—When her teenage son runs away from home because he is gay, Adele Star and twenty-four other concerned parents found Parents and Friends of Lesbians and Gays (P-FLAG).

February 25, 1982—Wisconsin becomes the first state to enact a gay rights law.

August, 1982—The first Gay Games is held in San Francisco.

April 30, 1983—Over 17,000 people flock to the Ringling Brothers, Barnum & Bailey Circus at Madison Square Garden to raise money for New York's Gay Men's Health Crisis.

July 14, 1983—Congressman Gerry Studds of Massachusetts

becomes the first Member of Congress to acknowledge his homosexuality in public.

November 6, 1984—Residents of West Hollywood, California vote to incorporate it as a separate city and elect three out of five gay members to the newly formed City Council.

October 2, 1985—Rock Hudson dies of complications associated with AIDS in Los Angeles.

October 21, 1985—Assassin Dan White commits suicide.

June 30, 1986—The Supreme Court upholds the constitutionality of state sodomy laws in *Hardwick v. Bowers*.

March, 1987—ACT UP (AIDS Coalition to Unleash Power) is formed to advocate increased federal government funding and action in the fight against AIDS.

May 7, 1987—Republican Stewart B. McKinney becomes the first U.S. congressman to die of AIDS-related complications. His widow later establishes a foundation to provide funding for AIDS-related services.

October 11, 1987—In the largest Gay Rights demonstration to date, more than a half million people participate in the Second March on Washington. That same weekend the Names Project unveils the entire AIDS Memorial Quilt on the Mall in the nation's capital.

March 29, 1988—The nation's oldest Catholic university, Georgetown, loses its battle to withhold financial support from gay student groups.

December 1, 1988—The World Health Organization holds the first World AIDS Day.

June 13, 1989—Washington's Corcoran Gallery of Art cancels a scheduled exhibit of photographs by Robert Mapplethorpe. Thousands later line up to see the show at the Washington Project for the Arts.

August, 1990—More than 7,000 athletes compete in the third Gay Games in Vancouver, Canada.

October 27, 1990—Congress repeals the federal law blocking gay and lesbian foreigners from entering the United States.

September 29, 1991—Pete Wilson, Republican Governor of California, vetoes gay rights legislation.

May 18, 1992—Candidate Clinton, addressing the gay and lesbian crowd at a Human Rights Campaign Fund fundraiser in Los Angeles, tells them, "I have a vision, and you are a part of it."

July 14, 1992—Openly gay and HIV+ presidential campaign worker Bob Hattoy addresses the Democratic National Convention in New York. A first.

January 20, 1993—William Jefferson Clinton is sworn in as the 42nd President of the United States. That night, gay men and lesbians celebrate their political clout at the first Triangle Inaugural Ball.

April 25, 1993—Several hundred thousand—perhaps a million—people participate in the third March on the nation's capital calling for gay and lesbian civil rights.

November 16, 1993—A three-judge panel of the U.S. Court of Appeals for the District of Columbia holds the military's ban on gays unconstitutional. The Clinton Administration appeals the ruling.

June 25–26, 1994—Thousands of gays and lesbians converge on New York City to commemorate the 25th anniversary of the Stonewall uprising.

"... [Y]ou cannot demand your rights, civil or otherwise, if you are unwilling to say what you are."

—MERLE MILLER, WRITER

PORK IS A VERB
A Lexicon

a few fries short of a Happy Meal *adj.* **1.** having a few screws loose; **2.** ditzy, as in, "That Greg is kind of cute, but I think he's *a few fries short of a Happy Meal.*"

angel food *n.* a pilot, a man in the Air Force (*See* **seafood.**)

attitude *n.* an air of aloof superiority, as in "The White Party was hot, but the *attitude* was a bit much," or "Sure, he's successful, but he has *so* much *attitude.*"

bar biography *n.* revisionist family or personal history, a false and inflated description of one's self, as in "He's a waiter, but according to his *bar biography* he's a stockbroker."

bear *n.* a hairy and often hefty man

beard *n.* a woman whom a gay man brings to events as a cover, to give the illusion that he is straight (becoming *Obs.*)

belle of the ball *n.* Queen Bee, a queen that always has to be the center of attention, often used derisively

bent *adj.* *British* for gay (becoming *Obs.*)

b.f. *n.* boyfriend

big girl *n.* a guy who, for all his attempts at *machismo,* is very effeminate. *syns.* big woman, big 'mo, big Mary

blonde *adj.* ditzy

bottom *n.* in bed, one who believes it is better to receive than to give

box *n.* for some, a man's calling card, located front and center, below the waist and above the knee. *syn.* basket

boy *n.* a gay man

boyfriend *n.* something between a friend and a lover; someone you're dating, but not quite ready to pick out a duvet cover with

boy toy *n.* young (18–22 years old) club kid, often seen wearing go-go outfits. *syn.* toy boy

breeder *n.* a heterosexual. *ant.* non-breeder

buddy *n.* a person who volunteers to help out a PWA with everyday chores and to be a companion to him or her

buffed *adj.* pumped up from exercise; *also* "buffed up"

bump *n.* one hit of a powdered drug, such as Special K, that can be snorted at once

bump and twirl *v.* to party

busy *adj.* flamboyant, nelly, as in "That outfit he had on was so *busy*," or "His friends are friendly, but they're a little *busy*."

butch *adj.* masculine

butch it up *v.* to try to act butch, as in "When my parents come to dinner, do you think you can cut the Patti LaBelle routine and try to *butch it up* just a little?"

camp *n.* exaggerated gestures, styles, and emotions that are humorous; *adj.* having camp characteristics, as in "*The Rocky Horror Picture Show* is so *camp*."

Canadian *adj.* gay

CD *n.* cute Daddy; usu. used to refer to an attractive man with children

CED *n.* Cosmetic Effect of Distance (Darkness), as in "At the bar, he looked like Mel Gibson, but once we got outside under a streetlight, I realized it must've been *CED;* he looked more like Hervé Villechaize."

chicken *n.* a young gay man, usu. slender and smooth

chickenhawk *n.* an older gay man who prefers chicken

children *n.* gay people, usu. used in African-American community

circuit *n.* the annual string of big dance parties in various locations, including the White Party(ies), Black Party, Hotlanta, and GMHC Morning Party

circuit queen *n.* one who does—no, lives for—the circuit

clone *n.* a gay man who sports an outfit and grooming traits that were made popular in New York and San Francisco in the seventies (*See* Chapter III.)

come out *v.* **1.** internally, to come to terms with and accept the fact that you're gay; **2.** externally, to stop hiding the fact that you're gay, and live all aspects of your life openly, in the same way that straight people do

cruise *v.t.* to gaze at someone with the intention of engaging his attention, and eventually talking to him (or more), as in "Maybe I'm hallucinating, but I swear that muscle boy at the gym was cruising me."; *v.i.* to go out looking for guys, as in "He spends every Sunday afternoon cruising Dupont Circle."

cut *adj.* **1.** having well-defined

muscles and little fat; **2.** circumcised; *ant.* uncut

Daddy *n.* an older man who is the object of a younger man's affection, often with the apparent means to support both of them in style. (*See* **sugar daddy, CD**.)

Dairy Queen *n.* a gay man that likes to suck on nipples. *syn.* unweaned queen

date *v.* to go out with someone *n.* one you begin an evening with, though may not end the evening with. (*Compare* **trick**.)

datette *n.* a mini-date, usu. without an overnight stay

delish *adj.* delicious. *also* **del**

dish *n.* gossip. *syn.* dirt, 411; *v.* to gossip

dish queen *n.* a queen who loves to—guess what—dish

"Don't ask, don't tell." *adj. phrase.* used to describe the policy adopted in 1993 to allow gays to serve in the military *if* they keep their sexual orientation a secret and do not engage in gay sex.

"Don't clutch your pearls." *command.* [from the opera diva's clutching her pearls when a musician hits a wrong note] Don't come unraveled; don't get worked up.

"Don't come for me." *command, warning.* Don't start talking about that subject, or you'll be sorry.

"Don't go there." *command, warning.* Don't come for me.

drag *n.* clothing, hair, and other affectations of a style that's not really your own, usu. that of a woman, but could also be biker *drag*, leather *drag*, cowboy *drag*, lawyer *drag*, etc.

drag queen *n.* a queen who enjoys, and maybe earns a living, doing drag

drama *n.* big, emotional personal turmoil, such as a relationship breaking up, a dinner party being crashed by a rude guest, and other travails; the makings of good gossip

drama queen *n.* a queen who loves to stir up the pot, who thrives on drama

evil queen *n.* a bitch

fabu (fa-*boo*) *adj.* fabulous

fag hag *n.* a straight woman who spends a lot of time with gay men (often considered a derisive term by fag hags themselves)

family *n. used as an adj.* a gay person, as in "Is he *family?*"

fierce (feersss) *adj.* great; the highest compliment that can be paid to a queen, as in, "I love RuPaul. She is *fierce.*"

fish *n.* (derogatory) a woman; *pl.* fish

flaming *adj.* flamboyantly effeminate, busy

fluffer *n.* in blue movies, one whose job it is to make sure the stars are up for their parts (or vice versa)

for days *adj.* galore, many, large, as in "That guy has arms *for days.*"

4-1-1 *n.* [from the phone number you dial for information] dish, information, as in "I've been away for a few days; give me the *4-1-1.*"

friend of Dorothy *n.* [from Judy Garland's character, Dorothy Ga(y)le in *The Wizard of Oz*] a gay person

fruitfly *n.* a fag hag

Gaydar *n.* the instinctual ability to ascertain that another guy is gay, even in the absence of telltale signs

"Get her!" *colloq.* Can you believe the nerve of that guy? Imagine that!

"Get over it." *command.* Put it behind you, stop talking about it. *Also:* **Get over yourself.** Stop being so self-centered.

get your tail done *v.* to have relations as a bottom

GIB *adj.* good in bed

girl *n.* man, sometimes used as a form of address, usu. between friends, as in "*Girl!*" or "Go, *girl!*"

girlfriend *n.* close gay friend; often used as a form of address as in "*Girlfriend!* You'll never believe what I heard!"

Girth & Mirth *n.* an organization for heavy-set gay men

glam *adj.* glamorous

grande (grahnd) *adj.* pretentious, having a lot of attitude, as in "Sabin may be wealthy, but he's too *grande* for my taste."

grower, not a shower *n.* one whose natural gifts are not immediately apparent, but become apparent with time and the right stimuli

gym bunny *n.* a guy who works out a lot and has a *great* body, but is very nelly. (*See* **See Tarzan, hear Jane.**)

hairdon't *n.* a bad hairdo

helium heels *n. used as adj. or nickname.* a bottom

herself *n.* himself

heterosexual privilege *n.* the right of non-gay persons to present an unedited version of their weekend activities to their co-workers and to place photos of their loved ones on their office desks without fear of repercussions

himself *n.* someone who is self-important. (*Compare:* **herself.**)

HIT *n.* homo in training, a young gay man who may or may not be aware that he's gay

house *n.* a gay gang, a close-knit

group of gay friends, usu. in the African-American community, often very structured, ruled by a mother, and often named after its founder, e.g., the "*House* of LaBeija"

hundred-dollar millionaire *n.* all flash, no cash

important *adj.* significant, particularly as enhancing one's social standing, at least in one's own mind, as in "Our new dining room can seat thirty for *important* dinner parties."

in the Life *adj.* gay, as in, "Is he *in the Life,* or just an artistic heterosexual?"

"It's over." *Adj. phrase.* It's tired, it's out of fashion.

K-hole *n.* a state of disorientation resulting from overindulgence in Special K (not the cereal), as in "She's been out of it for a while, but she'll be okay; she's just in a *K-hole.*"

lambda *n.* the Greek letter (λ) which has been a symbol of the Gay Rights movement since 1970: There are two explanations for its significance: first, it is the symbol for synergy, meaning that the whole is greater than the sum of its parts; second, it is the Greek equivalent of the letter "L," standing for "Lancôme"(or is it "liberation"?)

Lean Cuisine queen *n.* a queen who is always on a diet

leather queen *n.* a queen who's into leather drag

life jacket *n.* condom. *syns.* rubber, johnson cover, billet-doux, prophylactic, love glove, sleeve, wiener wrap, jimmy, raincoat, sombrero, pocket pal, rubber duckie, homey hood, umbrella

lover *n.* a longtime partner, someone you expect to spend the rest of your life with

lucky Pierre *n.* the third in a three-way with two lovers or boyfriends

Mary *n.* a gay man, usu. used as a form of address, as in, "*Mary!* Did I show you my new jacket?"

Mattachine Society *n.* a gay organization founded in L.A. in the early 1950s which advocated acceptance and understanding of, and equal rights for, gays

mean queen *n.* a queen who is into S & M

"Milk?" *n.* used to stop someone who is being catty

millionaire/model/genius *n.* a guy who's none of these, but says he is, or at least exaggerates his own importance

Miss Congeniality *n.* a bitch, as in "Turn around and don't look up; here comes *Miss Congeniality* herself."

Miss Thing *n.* a title or form of address for a nelly, flamboyant, or haughty gay man, as in "Did you see *Miss Thing* driving up and down Santa Monica with the top down on her new Miata and her chiffon scarf blowing in the wind?"

'mo *n.* [from homo] a gay man

MOMD *n.* Man of My Dreams

mother *n.* the Queen Bee, particularly an African-American queen who heads up a group of men, usu. younger than herself, and often in a formalized house (*See* **house**)

muffin *n.* a gay man, esp. a cute one

muscle muffin *adj.* a muffin with muscles, usu. a short man

Nancy *n.* a big woman

NAWW *adj.* Not a Well Woman

nelly *adj.* effeminate

nellyectomy *n.* an imaginary operation in which a bone is removed from the wrist, giving it greater flexibility, and in which other changes are made to a man to make him more nelly, as in "He is the butchest thing at work, but the minute he walks into a bar, it's as if he's had a *nellyectomy*—those hands start flailing and that voice rises three octaves."

"No, she didn't!" *colloq.* You don't say! Used to express surprise

on fire *adj.* flaming, as in "That queen's *on fire.*"

only good for the 3 gets *adj.* good only for quick, unemotional sex, having no other redeeming value, as in "He was *only good for the 3 gets.*" (*See* **the 3 gets**.)

openly gay *adj.* a heterosexual term for one who has come out, who isn't ashamed to wear Gay Pride T-shirts in the presence of straight people, and doesn't try to pretend that he's not gay (Oft. used derogatorily)

orphan *n.* one whose lover has dumped him

Peter Pan *n.* a fictional character, often believed to depict a gay man, who, when he realized that his parents wanted him to grow up, get married, and have children, fled to Never, Never Land to live with a group of lost boys and a jealous fairy named Tinkerbell

PiB *n.* Person in Black

pig *n.* a slut

pink triangle *n.* a symbol of the Gay Rights movement, always with point facing down, having originated in Nazi concentration camps as the symbol worn by those interred and killed for being gay

poppers *n.* originally, amyl nitrate; now, usually refers to butyl nitrate, a volatile liquid sold as "room deodorizer" (becoming *Obs.*). Anyone who's ever smelled it knows no one would ever want his room to smell like that. When inhaled, it causes increased heart rate and blood pressure and disorientation. Nasty stuff.

pork *v.i.* to have sex; *v.t.* to be an active top

prec' (presh) *adj.* precious, often used to demean, as in, "Aren't those kneesocks *prec'* on him?"

Prince Albert *n.* a pierced popo

princess *n.* a queen in the making

PT *n.* profile trap; being deceivingly attractive only from the side

pushing box *v.* arranging oneself to accentuate one's natural gifts, or compensating with artificial devices (e.g., socks) for what nature failed to provide

put [one's] foot in the pot *v.* to cook a delicious meal, as in "That was the best chili I ever tasted! You really *put your foot in the pot.*"

PWA *n.* a person living with AIDS

queen *n.* **1.** a flamboyant, nelly gay man; **2.** any gay man

Queen Bee *n.* a queen who always has to be the center of attention; a control freak

queen for a day *n.* a married man who sometimes plays around with guys

Queen of Denial *n.* not Cleopatra, but a queen who can't or won't admit something, usually to herself, such as the fact that she's a shopoholic, as in "All my credit cards are over their limits, but I'll find the money to go to Hawaii. Oh, I am *such* a *Queen of Denial.*"

queen without a country *n.* a queen who does a lousy job at being a queen, e.g., she dresses shabbily, thinks she's witty but isn't, or fancies herself popular, but isn't

Quilt, the *n.* a huge commemorative quilt comprising over two thousand panels, each of which is six by three feet and is a memorial to at least one person who has died of AIDS-related complications. Although each panel has been made by friends and loved ones of those who have died, the coordination of the creation and exhibition of the Quilt has been the work of the Names Project.

rainbow, rainbow flag *n.* Originally a symbol of the 1978 San Francisco Gay Freedom Parade representing the diversity of the gay community, the rainbow and rainbow flag have been adopted as symbols of the entire gay movement.

read *v.t.* to insult someone with a torrent of usually true statements about the person, often in front of other people, as in "I had to *read* that salesman right then and there in Better Sportswear." *Also:* read [his] beads.

reading *n.* a major series of insults, as in "Get out your library card; I'm about to give this girl a serious *reading*."

ret 2 go *adj.* ready to go

rodent *n.* a gay man

S & M bar *n.* stand and model bar, a bar frequented by pretty boys who stand around posing aloofly

safe *adj.* not likely to allow sexually transmitted diseases to spread

safe sex *n.* sexual relations where the participants take precautions to prevent the spread of sexually transmitted diseases, particularly HIV

seafood *n.* a sailor, a man in the Navy

See Tarzan, hear Jane. *adj. phrase.* a guy with a great body who turns out to be nelly, with a nelly voice, usu. a disappointment

shade *n.* attitude

shady *adj.* having a lot of shade

she *pron.* he

significant other *n.* lover, a term which originated with gays and (like many others) has been adopted by straights

sings in the choir *adj.* is gay, in the Life. *syn.* goes to our church

sister *n.* fellow gay man

size queen *n.* a gay man who emphasizes mass over motion

skag drag *n.* female drag where no attempt is made to hide masculine characteristics, resulting in one ugly woman

sleaze *n.* someone sleazier than yourself

"Slow down, Mary." *colloq.* You're out of line.

smooth *adj.* shaved of all body hair

snow queen *n.* a gay who uses cocaine

SOS trip *n.* Shopping-and-Other-Sins trip

Stonewall *n.* the riot early in the morning of June 28, 1969 (the day after Judy Garland was buried) at the Stonewall Inn in Greenwich Village where, after being the victims of numerous police raids, the men at this gay establishment finally fought back; the beginning of the modern Gay Rights movement

sugar daddy *n.* an older man of means who supports a younger man of motives

tea dance *n.* an afternoon dance, often outside, and usually held on Sunday, started at the Blue Whale on Fire Island in 1966

tearoom *n.* a public restroom

the 123 words *n.* the policy of the U.S. armed forces from 1981 to 1993, which prohibited gay men and lesbians from serving their country

"the pink part" *command.* Kiss my butt.

the 3 gets *n.* get home, get off, get out, usu. used in the phrase "only good for *the 3 gets*"

throw shade *v.* to give attitude

tired *adj.* boring, used to refer to events, places, and people

Titanic *adj.* awesome, incredible

to die for *adj.* wonderful, fabulous, as in "His chest was *to die for.*"

top *n.* in bed, one who believes it is better to give than to receive

trade *n.* a hustler, the state of being a hustler, as in "Have you ever noticed how that new boyfriend of Charles's knows *everyone* in the bar? That's because he's *done* everyone in the bar. He's *trade.*"

Tragicula *n.* a person with a tragic life, or poor taste in hair, clothes, etc.

trick *n.* someone you end the evening with, but did not start the evening with, i.e., not a date; *v.* to sleep with a trick

trickmeister *n.* a whore

troll *n.* an unattractive older man

twirled *adj.* **1.** worked up; **2.** under the influence of drugs

vanity smurf *n.* a person who is constantly checking himself out in a mirror, often seen at the gym

vogue *v.* [from the fashion magazine] to dance in a precise, measured way, mimicking a fashion model's moves and poses, often competitively against other voguers

wannabe *n.* a self-proclaimed straight man who is curious about the gay world, and may eventually become a part of it

woman *n.* a queen, a very effeminate man

work *v.t.* **1.** to network with an agenda, as in "He *worked* the room, trying to get people to buy his book"; **2.** to flirt with someone: "Did you see how that troll *worked* my boyfriend?"

work it *v.* to show off, flaunt; often used as a command, as in "*Work it,* girl!"

work [one's] last nerve *v.* to provoke or agitate someone, as in "You'd better stop asking me my name every time we meet. You're *working my last nerve.*"

worked *adj.* agitated, worked up, as in "He got so *worked* when he saw me out with his ex."

X queen *n.* a queen who takes a lot of Ecstasy ("XTC")

"You better . . ." *Adj. phrase.* used as a compliment, meaning "You're good at [fill in the blank]." Made famous by RuPaul's "*You better* work!" which meant "You're good at working it," *not* "You'd better get a job."

BIBLIOGRAPHY
and Recommendations
for Further Reading

The Alyson Almanac: The Fact Book of the Lesbian and Gay Community, 1994–95 ed. Boston: Alyson Publications, Inc., 1993.

The Big Gay Book: A Man's Survival Guide for the 90's. Edited by John Preston. New York: Penguin Books USA Inc., 1991.

Bronski, Michael. *Culture Clash: The Making of Gay Sensibility.* Boston: South End Press, 1984.

Damron Address Book '94. San Francisco: The Damron Company, 1994.

Fletcher, Lynne Yamaguchi, and Adrien Saks. *Lavender Lists: New Lists About Lesbian and Gay Culture, History, and Personalities.* Boston: Alyson Publications, Inc., 1990.

Gay Life: Leisure, Love, and Living for the Contemporary Gay Male. Edited by Eric E. Rofes. Garden City, New York: Doubleday & Company, Inc., 1986.

Greif, Martin. *The Gay Book of Days: An Evocatively Illustrated Who's Who of Who Is, Was, May Have Been, Probably Was, and Almost Certainly Seems to Have Been Gay During the Past 5,000 Years.* New York: Carol Publishing Group, 1982.

Halliwell, Leslie. *Halliwell's Film Guide,* 5th ed. New York: Charles Scribner's Sons, 1987.

Marcus, Eric. *Is It a Choice?: Answers to 300 of the Most Frequently Asked Questions About Gays and Lesbians.* San Francisco: Harper-Collins Publishers, 1993.

Out & About, various issues, 1992–1994.

Roen, Paul. *High Camp: A Gay Guide to Camp and Cult Films.* Vol. 1. San Francisco: Leyland Publications, 1994.

Rutledge, Leigh W. *The Gay Book of Lists.* Boston: Alyson Publications, Inc., 1987 (4th printing, 1992).

Rutledge, Leigh W. *The Gay Decades: From Stonewall to the Present: The People and Events That Shaped Gay Lives.* New York: Penguin Books USA Inc., 1992.

Rutledge, Leigh W. *The Gay Fireside Companion.* Boston: Alyson Publications, Inc., 1989.

Rutledge, Leigh W. *Unnatural Quotations.* Boston: Alyson Publications, Inc., 1988.

Stewart, Steve. *Gay Hollywood Film & Video Guide: Over 75 Years of Male Homosexuality in the Movies.* Laguna Hills: Companion Publications, 1993.